PRAISE FOR THE FIRST EDITION OF *START NOW*

"WOW! Reading *Start Now* really gave me renewed encouragement about today's youth. Jason Abell sincerely wants to bring out the absolute best, personally and financially, in anyone who reads his book. If every young adult could read Jason's ground breaking, passionate writing today, the world would certainly be full of much needed leaders tomorrow."
—Roger Dawson
Author, *Secrets of Power Negotiating*

"For anyone who is committed to their long-term success, Jason Abell's book, *Start Now* is the best place for information that is practical, profound, easily applicable, and fun to read."
—Patricia Fripp
Past President, National Speakers Association, Author, *Get What You Want*

"In 26 years of doing news and talk-show interviews, I've never talked with anyone who had better advice for young people than Jason Abell! His book *Start Now* is superb."
—Steve Simon
Radio Talk-Show Host and Producer

"A cutting-edge book in the field! Any young person reading *Start Now* will have a critical edge in personal and professional development."
—Joseph Procaccini
Professor, Loyola College in Maryland, Leadership and Decision Making
Author of several books on parenthood

"Jason's book *Start Now* is an exceptionally motivating book in which people can quickly take action to create the career success they want to realize their dreams. The success steps that Jason outlines in the book are clear and absolutely necessary to achieve success. *Start Now* is a must for anyone starting out and I strongly recommend this book for anyone who wishes to have career and life success."
—Anne Boe
International Keynote Speaker, Author, *Is Your "Net" Working?*

"*Start Now* is about self-mastery and discipline. I am overjoyed to see Jason Abell taking a real stand on these issues for the betterment of young adults and our society. I strongly feel that everyone will benefit greatly from heeding to Jason's techniques. The fact that he is so young gives me hope that America still has a chance to restore forgotten discipline.
—Jhoon Rhee
Founder and President, The World Martial Arts Congress for Education

"Jason's mature sense of abundance enables the reader to employ the lessons of *Start Now* from the vantage point of "give-it-all-you-got" rather than "take-all-you-can-get." People in every age range and at every stage of their journey will benefit from the wise reflections in this most valuable book."
—Emily C. Thayer
Founder and Executive Director, Genesis Jobs, Inc.

START NOW

START NOW

THE YOUNG ADULT'S PASSPORT TO SUCCESS AND WELL-BEING

Jason Abell

RED LIZARD PRESS

Published by: Red Lizard Press. West Linn, Oregon.

Printed in the United States.

Library of Congress Control Number:2019953448

ISBN 978-0-9970174-8-9

Start Now: A Young Adult's Passport to Success and Well-Being/Jason Abell

THIS BOOK IS DEDICATED TO YOU—
THE YOUTHFUL READER

CONTENTS

INTRODUCTION

THE *WHY* BEHIND THIS BOOK

"Youth is not a time of life, but a state of mind... a predominance of courage over timidity, of the appetite for adventure over love of ease... it does not accept failures of today but knows it can grasp the future and mold it to our will."

—ROBERT F. KENNEDY

While sitting in a computer class at Loyola College in Baltimore on April 10, 1991 (gasp!—such a long time ago!), I began to jot down little hints and secrets I had learned that seemed to give me a bit of an edge over my fellow students. I wrote down ideas on the importance of goal setting, organization, discipline, and diversity. It quickly become clear to me that learning techniques such as proper time and money management, communication skills, and relational skills at a young age is the passport for success as the journey of life rolls on. I also realized that because many of my friends at the time didn't know much about and/or understand these concepts, they weren't able to make them a regular practice.

When I was still a teenager, I was fortunate enough to be exposed to great financial teachers such as Jimmy Napier, John Schaub, and Roger Dawson (you may have never heard of these guys—look them up, they're awesome). Along with this exposure, my father's home library provided more motivational books and tapes (yes, cassette tapes!) than I could shake a stick at. My father assured me that these materials were available to me whenever I desired to study them. We're talking about thought leaders such as Zig Ziglar, John Maxwell, Dale Carnegie, Tony Robbins, Napoleon Hill, and the like. I quickly found out through experience and observation that these teachers, books, and tapes held the secrets to getting ahead in life, both financially and personally.

But there was a problem! And the problem was that this information seemed to be available only to older generations. I guess that's why I called it "secret." Most of the material contained in this book is not taught in schools, even today. Not that any of it is difficult. As a matter of fact, most of the material is surprisingly, almost laughably, easy to follow!

But back to that long ago computer class. About ten minutes into writing down these hints, I decided that somehow I *had* to make this information available to others my age. It didn't seem fair to me that these secrets don't typically get into the hands of the young. We were the ones who could make the best use of this information if we were able to implement it properly. I couldn't sleep that night, and at 3:58 the next morning I began writing the first edition of this book.

Today is January 15, 2019, and we are in the thick of updating this book for you, today's youth. When I originally wrote it, I was in the same age bracket as you are now and the ideas were not coming from any kind of so-called "authority," but rather from what would have been a peer. I purposefully finished this book while I was twenty-one and still in college because I believed that it would have a greater effect coming from an equal instead of someone in "authority." I felt compelled to share some of the secrets that had worked for me up to that point in my life. Unlike most people who have had to break bad habits when they get older, the readers of *Start Now* would be inspired to "start now" with the habits that create success.

Let me get your inspirational juices flowing by clueing you in on some of what I was able to accomplish using the secrets I was then writing about: I created a passive income in excess of $10,000 a year for myself before graduating from college; I put my financial life in order and was prepared to take on post-collegiate financial responsibilities; I'd made friends and associates from all walks of life; I was often asked for advice on diverse subjects ranging from relationships to finances; and I developed clear-cut goals for the future, many of which have since been realized.

I don't relate these accomplishments to toot my own horn, but rather to show you the types of things you can achieve, at whatever age you are right now, if you really put your mind to it. As a matter of fact, I sincerely hope that your accomplishments far surpass mine. The greatest gift I could receive would be some sort of communication from you that relates the ways this book helped you in life, either financially or personally.

Beside the fact that I am now well into my forties, and probably, by most accounts (other than Robert Kennedy's of course), not considered a youth anymore, the reason for the existence of this book is the same as it was decades ago: to share information that will set you on the right road, personally and financially, at a much earlier age than most people experience it.

The world, however, is a different place than it was in 1991. For instance, in 1991 the internet was hardly even around and certainly not available in many households. Today, most of us carry the internet around in our pocket. The last few decades have seen many female thought leaders emerge that I'm incredibly grateful for such as Brené Brown, Jen Sincero, Marie Forleo, and Emily P. Freeman. What is not different today are the topics I began to write about when I was nineteen. Having amazing friends who push and help you, the importance of individualism and human relations, and your relationship with money, goals, and discipline may be even more important today than ever before. So here I am with more than twenty-five years of experience that include mistakes (failed businesses, missed opportunities, faded relationships, a risk or two that were not, perhaps, that well thought out) and some successes (an amazing family, an abundance of business success, bonded relationships, and a self-awareness that continues to grow even as I type these words). These experiences are in my rearview mirror and I remain as passionate now as I ever was to get the information contained in this book into your hands.

When I was originally writing this book, I said that I was not an authority on many of the topics contained on these pages. That has changed a bit due to my experiences and the fact that people regularly seek out my advice on these topics. Over the last twenty-five plus years, I have done my best to put these techniques into play in my own life to see if they stood the test of time. I can confidently say that they do indeed!

I have been able to surround myself with some out-of-sight friends who have helped me not only accomplish some amazing things, but have just plain old been there for me when I've needed them the most. I've practiced the individualism techniques from chapter one, and they helped me live against the grain of society and achieve both business and personal well-being. I personally tested out the million-dollar plan outlined in chapter thirteen and I am happy to announce that it actually works in real life! Just last week, I filled out a personal net worth sheet for a line of credit we are requesting for our business, and my net worth was greater than two million dollars. I tell you none of this to brag, but rather to inspire you to fully understand that this stuff really works.

And my deep desire is that you use that understanding to take real, tangible, rubber-meets-the-road action in your own life to achieve results for yourself that otherwise may seem out of reach. I want to make available to you tools for getting ahead in life. How you decide to use them is entirely up to you.

Here's what else you need to know as you stand at the precipice of starting now:

1) My father's library mentioned above is still as available today to me and my nine siblings as it was in 1991 and I still "check out" materials from it from time to time. With the advent of YouTube and Audible, and of course your local library, you also have a massive library available to you. Use it! When you are working out or driving or doing the dishes, listen to a book or a podcast, or watch a YouTube video teaching you something you are interest in learning, or that will be helpful to you as you navigate your world. Just yesterday, my son, JJ, used YouTube to learn the finer points of tuning up our bicycles. I'm happy to report that he did an amazing job and saved us a few hundred dollars in the act. Before you go to bed, instead of social media, read a book. I promise you will be better for it.

2) I had some serious help with the revised edition of this book you now hold in your hands. I'm connected enough to know that my being in my mid-forties automatically disconnects me from certain aspects of your experience as a young adult. To bridge the gap, I enlisted eight young adults ranging in age from thirteen to twenty-eight. These amazing people read the original version of the book and, after making fun of some of my 1990s' vernacular, gave great suggestions for the changes needed to bring the book up-to-date. I think you'll appreciate their revisions.

3) You'll notice that we jump from topic to topic in this book. That is done on purpose because I want you to have exposure to all the information I was exposed to at a young age. There is a rhyme to this reason and even though we do indeed skip around a bit, the book as a whole is divided into three intentional sections: how we engage others, how we engage ourselves, and how we engage money. Then, there is a smaller section at the end, just to wrap things up.

The order of these sections is important; I want you to focus on others first and then, and only then, turn to take a close look at yourself. We end with your relationship with money. There are so many other places I could have gone with this book, but those three, in that particular order, feels right to me in terms of how it may add the most value to you.

4) One last thing: The more we learn about the brain due to technological advances in the medical field, the more appreciation I have for the fact that no matter what you read in this book and no matter what works for me or anyone else you read about, you will need to pick and choose what works for YOU: YOUR personality, YOUR gifted zone, YOUR desires, and YOUR uniqueness. YOUR own path in life is what is important: what YOU desire in life and how YOU want to get there. So when you see the word "success" in the title or written throughout this book, I want to make clear before you read any further that my definition of success for you is whatever YOUR definition of success is for yourself. YOUR unique path that you carve out for YOURSELF is what's amazing, and it is the real definition of success.

To this end, at the end of each chapter, I've asked "What will YOU do as a result of reading this chapter?" and then for "YOUR Thoughts on ______." I encourage you to keep a journal handy and to write down your thoughts on what you just read before moving on to the next topic. Spend a little time thinking through each topic and mapping out any specific actions you are going to take. Make this book and its topics your own and do amazing things with it.

That's it for now. Let's dig in and do this thing.

Let's Start Now!

SECTION ONE:

HOW WE ENGAGE OTHERS

CHAPTER ONE

INDIVIDUALISM

In my opinion, you should never strive to be a part of the crowd or led to think something is right just because everyone else thinks it is. Many people think that if they just dress or act like most other people, they will fit in with the rest of the world and everything will just fall into place. The problem with this thinking is that things don't fall into place, at least not the way we would like them to. You see, many people aren't doing very smart things these days, especially financially. So, those who attempt to follow this "norm" in dealing with their money, for example, will likely find that they will not be able to support themselves during the "golden" retirement years.

Wait a minute here Jason! I'm still a kid; why are you talking to me about retirement?

No, I don't want you to go out and set up a retirement fund for yourself just yet, but retirement is something that should at least be in the back of your mind from the beginning these days.

But why?

Because, if you keep putting off the thought, one day you'll be left without much money, wealth, or legacy. You'll be stuck and wishing you had considered the matter a little earlier in life.

Enough on retirement for now. What I am asking you to do in this chapter isn't that difficult. I want you not to be afraid to be an individual. I'm encouraging you with everything I've got to rise above the crowd and be you. There is only one of you in this world—just one. You are on this earth for a very specific reason. You may not know what that reason is just yet, but I can assure you, that reason does not include you just being like everyone else. In college, my sophomore philosophy professor told our class to make sure we weren't part of the herd because the herd was often headed for the slaughterhouse! He was trying to tell us to think for ourselves instead of sitting back and accepting what we were told. It's a pretty simple idea, and it makes sense, too. It's not necessarily easy to implement in our everyday lives, but that's precisely why this topic made it into this book. I want to plant this individualism seed into your brain now in hopes that over time it will take root, and germinate into you being your own self and bringing to the world what only you can bring to it.

Each and every one of us is a unique entity. No two people in this world of well over seven billion are exactly alike, nor will there ever be two people exactly alike. Some people, as I said before, try their hardest to be like others so they will fit in. But doing so ignores their uniqueness. Please don't hide your uniqueness by conforming to others. Be your distinctive self and be proud of it. No matter which side of the tracks you come from, you should be proud, never ashamed or embarrassed. I don't care whether you're black, white, yellow or red; female or male; Asian, German, Irish, African or Latin American; Hindu, Jewish, Catholic or Episcopalian; ten, twenty-two, or eighty-nine; a high school graduate, college graduate or no graduate at all; inflicted with a life-threatening disease or healthy as a horse. You are who you are, and a higher being made you that way for very specific reasons.

You are unique and special, so own it. Nonconformity is the quality that separates us from the rest of creation. Let's make sure we maintain our individuality.

THE 95 PERCENT RULE

Jimmy Napier, one of my mentors, first taught me about money with the 95 percent rule, which simply states that you should do the exact opposite of whatever 95 percent of the population is doing financially. At first glance this idea may seem a little odd, but allow me to explain. You see, many, possibly even most, of the people in this country are not happy with their present financial situation. If you put your money where most other people do because you believe that if you stick with the status quo your money will be well spent or safe, you are 100 percent wrong. If ninety-five out of every one hundred people jump off a bridge, would you follow suit, thinking it must be right because most everyone is doing it? If your answer is yes, please stop reading this book right now; it won't do you any good anyway. If your answer is no, stand against gravity and read on.

A perfect example is the credit card situation today. The way many people shop around for credit cards is to find one that charges a low annual percentage rate. The reason behind this is that 43 percent of the people who have credit cards carry a balance each month and therefore must pay the rate charged (https://www.lexingtonlaw.com/blog/loans/credit-card-debt-statistics.html).

As you will see in chapter fifteen, my strong advice to you is that if you've decided to have a card, make absolutely sure you pay off your total balance each month. That way you won't have to worry about what interest rate your credit card company charges because you'll never pay it. You'll also be building credit and discipline, both of which we also cover in later chapters of this book. Does this go against the grain of most people? Yes. Are you losing out or being penalized because of it? No. Instead, you're gaining because you will never have to pay the high interest rates, and you'll have the opportunity to benefit from the rewards many cards offer. See my point?

USE IT EVERYWHERE

THE 95 PERCENT rule does not apply to financial situations alone. One day, as I was typing a business email, one of my roommates at Loyola was looking over my shoulder, and he was quick to point out that I only had three lines between the address and the salutation. He said that I most definitely would need to change it to six lines. I asked him why. He said that it was the correct way to do it and that it was the standard. When I heard that buzzword, "standard," I quickly realized that I absolutely had to change it to six lines. NOT! It's not as if my message wouldn't get through if I didn't change it. So I left it. My email got to its destination just fine and the recipient was so happy to get the information I sent her that she didn't even notice my incorrect format for a business email. Boy, was I lucky!

Yeah, I know. That example was given with some sarcasm, but my hope is that you are starting to hear my point about individualism. You will positively get further in this world when you do not always conform to everyone else's norms and standards. Remember, just because everyone is doing it one way does not necessarily make it the right way.

Granted, there are times when it is common courtesy to do things the way most people do them. Or maybe it just makes more sense for you at the time. For example, when you go to a party and you know that the dress is formal, it probably isn't a good idea to show up in jeans. I mean you can, but I wouldn't really suggest it. In cases like that, it is best that you use your own judgment, listening to your gut feeling on the topic. I'm sure there are those who could make a case that my email above is an example of a time when I should have just conformed to the norm. They may have a valid case, but after what my roommate said, I just couldn't do it the "standard" way.

Your individualism can be used, celebrated, and is needed in every aspect of your life, ranging from the professional you to the personal you to you as a sibling, athlete, student, young adult, friend, advocate, gamer, or anything else you can think of that describes you.

GREATNESS

It is not easy being a nonconformist, but it leads to greatness. Think of any person you look up to or think of as great, for whatever reason. Maybe you have a certain teacher in mind, a professional athlete, a singer, or maybe even a parent or grandparent. If that person were like everyone else, a "conformist," would you still think of that person as being great?

Take a minute to really think about the above question before moving on to the next paragraph.

If that person did not possess a certain unique quality that made them stand out from the crowd in some regard, they would not stand out in your mind as being great. A person can't be like everyone else and still be extraordinary. If they were, it would contradict the very definition of greatness, which is that which is beyond the ordinary.

Heck, think about yourself in this context for a moment. Think about a time in your life when someone noticed you for something positive, or someone gave you a compliment, or maybe you won an award. Get the picture of that time in your mind's eye for a minute right now. Make the picture big and bright and really bring it into focus. Now, why were you noticed? Why did you receive that compliment or earn that award? Did it have something to do with you being just like everyone else, or were you standing out from the crowd in some way?

I want you to know that this practice applies to your financial life as well as many other aspects of your life such as your study or work habits. When a friend and subsequent manager of mine, Rick, helped to teach me the art of mortgage banking, he continuously stressed the importance of always looking for ways to "separate yourself from the others." He tried to get me to understand that success doesn't come from being *like* the others, but rather from being as *unlike* them as possible. And his personal success proved just how right he was. You see, when Rick was teaching me this lesson, he was in his mid-twenties and was well on his way to being one of the most respected mortgage bankers in the Washington, DC, metropolitan area. And now, at the time of my writing this update, some twenty-five years later, Rick serves as the president of both a well-respected company in the mortgage industry and a large industry association. As I've stated above, you don't get to that level of distinction by simply doing what everyone else does, but rather doing the opposite. Thanks, Rick. I very much appreciate that early education to this day.

As you experiment with your individualism, you will find that, although sometimes difficult, you actually like it. You will also find that others will begin to take notice of you and follow your example. At first you may face opposition as others compare your outward actions to what everyone else is doing. But as time passes, people will start looking up to you for having the courage to be an individual, and they may even start to do the same.

Wouldn't you rather be a leader in this world, displaying individualism and your unique you-ness, than be lumped in with the masses as a follower?

Go ahead and really take some time to think about the above question. It isn't there just to fill up the page, but rather for you to ponder for a minute. The fact that you are even reading this book suggests that leading is more your forte. What do you think?

START NOW!

What will YOU do as a result of reading this chapter?
YOUR Thoughts on Individualism.

CHAPTER TWO

FRIENDS

You MAY HAVE heard this before, but it is worth repeating, and then repeating again until you continually and consistently act on it. Make a habit of hanging around with people who make you better. One thing I have observed over and over again in life is this: You become the sum parts of the people you surround yourself with.

For instance, if one of your main goals in life is to become a real estate investor, but you don't hang around with anyone who knows anything about real estate, your chances of actually becoming a real estate investor are slim. I am not suggesting that you use people to get what you want, but rather am encouraging you to do what you need to do to be around these people to learn from them.

You may already do this without even realizing it. For example, if you wanted to learn to play basketball, what would you do? You would probably start to play pick-up games with your friends or join a basketball team. Automatically, you would have put yourself in a position to associate with people who also want to learn about and/or play the game. See how easy it is?

Hold the phone right here, Jason. You just finished telling me in the first chapter that I should never strive to be part of the crowd. Now you're telling me to hang around with people who have similar goals, tastes, etc. When people hang around each other, they eventually become a crowd. Are you saying that it is beneficial for me to be part of a crowd or not?

Great question, and I understand your concern. Let me clear things up a bit. Again, you are a unique individual and never should do anything just like someone else for the sole reason that "everyone is doing it." This line of thinking will eventually ruin your uniqueness. But if you are striving for a goal or something meaningful in your life that others already have accomplished or desire to accomplish, you're going to want to be around them. This way you can stimulate one another and grow together. And remember this: Just like most of life, the answer to the question above lies in the world of *and* not in the world of *or*. In other words, there are certain times, depending on context, when the answer for you is to run away from the crowd as fast as you can and there are other times when it will be most beneficial to you to purposefully seek out others.

Think of it this way: There are certain traits, characteristics, experiences, and histories of CEOs of companies. If you desire to lead a company yourself one day, it is a really good idea to spend time with people who have those leadership qualities and experiences, and maybe find ways to be around people who are currently leading companies. Join entrepreneurship clubs. Use Twitter or other social media to connect with leaders. Let everyone around you, like family, teachers, coaches, existing friends, and everyone else in your circle of influence, know that you want to be connected with other existing or aspiring leaders. Before you know it, little by little, you will be in contact with other leaders, possibly even CEOs. Spending time with people who have already walked the path you want to walk will help you find out if you really have what it takes to be a CEO one day, and it may cut down the CEO learning curve and possibly help you avoid some of the mistakes that others have made along the way.

I hope you see how this is entirely different from conforming with a crowd just because you are afraid to express your individualism. So in further answering the question above: "no" to joining a group if you are merely conforming to conform, and "yes" to joining a group if you are specifically trying to improve yourself and your skills or help others improve their skills. It is more a question of intent than anything else. If your intent is to go with the crowd just to fit in and it's the easy thing to do, then no dice. But if your intent is to be around like-minded individuals to drive success or toward a place you would like to be, yep!

FRIENDS = YOU

My grandmother used to say, "Jason, show me your friends and I'll tell you things about yourself that you probably don't think I know." And she would proceed to do just that. If you ever want to know why you are doing certain things, take a look at your friends and you will surely find the answer. I first read the following from Tim Ferriss, of *The 4-Hour Workweek* fame: We are the average of the five people we hang around with the most.

When I was seventeen, I began doing a substantial amount of maintenance on my parents' automobiles. The reason I was able to do that is not because I was a mechanic or went to school to work on cars, but was because I had the opportunity to learn from my buddy, Alex, who worked on cars at a local gas station. Often I would pick up Alex after work and he would be in the middle of repairing someone's car. I would watch and sometimes help him until the job was done. If I had never known Alex, I am sure those repairs on my parents' cars would not have been done by me, but rather by a mechanic at a repair shop. So I guess I saved my parents some money. Pretty nice of me, huh?

A friend's influence is so strong that it cannot be avoided. It just happens. In the above example, I wasn't purposely trying to learn auto mechanics; it just happened. Either you are going to make a conscious decision to be around people who share similar goals and tastes with you, or you will begin to unconsciously pick up the goals and tastes of the people you just happen to be around. Your community helps to shape the things you do and the choices you make, and I don't want them to happen for you by accident. Instead, shape and nurture them consciously by being mindful of the community you are choosing to be a part of. You can and should direct your goals and your focus instead of letting them be directed for you.

PEER PRESSURE

Jason, I'm starting to get this friend stuff, but what do I do if my current friends are negative influences on me? How do I escape?

Do that. Escape. Run. Flee. Say goodbye and don't look back. Influences can be either positive or negative, and peer pressure, which we all must deal with regularly, is a great example of just how strong these influences can really be. My auto mechanic example happened to be positive. A negative example could be alcoholism. If a person has a problem with alcohol and seeks help, one of the first things he is told to do is to stop associating with his circle of drinking friends. That is because those friends hold such a strong influence on that person. So if you aren't very happy with yourself, or even some small aspect of yourself, take a look at the people with whom you spend most of your time and you may find the answer to your unhappiness.

"Birds of a feather flock together." I'd be willing to bet that some of you have grandparents who have spoken that little phrase once or twice. I don't want you to get stuck in the wrong crowd and feel there is no way out because of the pressure. Get "stuck" in the right crowd for you from the start and your worries about negative pressures will drastically subside. Those negatives will never go away completely because the world is not a perfect place. Life would be boring without some of them anyway. But you can diminish them to make your life a little easier. In fact, one of my main goals in writing this book is to make your life just a little easier, to stack the deck in your favor a bit.

That would make my life easier, but am I just supposed to drop the friends I have because they are negative influences on me? They are the only friends I have. Who else would I hang out with?

If you truly think that your friends are bringing you down and want to move in a different direction, you are going to have to make the tough decision to get away from them. Don't delay the difficult and necessary inevitable. Sure, this is a hard thing to do and the transition period can be a very tough time in your life, but when you do make it through, you will come out a much better person. And be ready! This transition time might seem like an eternity, but I can assure you that in the big picture that is your life, it will be a minor blip and over before you know it.

While I was at a seminar in Florida one October, I met Joe, who had recently graduated from college. Joe told me that he'd graduated the past May with a degree in marketing. He said his job search wasn't going well at all until he read an article that I had written that said that you must drop your present friends if they are holding you back from what you want in life. You see, Joe wanted a job badly, but he would go out just about every night of the week with his drinking buddies and would not be in any kind of shape to be out the next day looking for a job, let alone perform in a successful interview. He told me that after reading my article he immediately stopped going out drinking with his buddies, even though he knew he would take a lot of flak from them about not doing it. The week following that decision, he had three interviews set up and another two for the week after that! Those five interviews were more than he'd had altogether since graduation. And yes, you guessed it. Joe secured himself a job shortly thereafter. Nice!

SCHOOL FRIENDS

Don't underestimate the importance of the friends you make in high school or college. Some of the friends I made while in school have become lifelong and precious people to me as the years have progressed. These are people with whom I still share very close, invaluable friendships. If I'm having a problem or a particularly hard time, sometimes the best therapy for me is to hang out with a few of my high school buddies. Because they've known me for so long, they know the important things about me without needing to be told. They make me feel relaxed and love and respect me like no one else. It's very comforting and safe.

Make sure you actively appreciate these friends as much as you can so you don't lose them. They really are precious and should never be taken for granted. True friends become an integral part of your life and can stay that way for a lifetime.

DIVERSIFIED ASSOCIATES

I AM ABOUT to tell you something that is seemingly contrary to what I have spent the last few pages talking about, so please read on with an open mind.

While I still want you to have friends who share your interests and goals, I also want you to have diversity in your associations with people. Don't limit yourself to those "real estate" friends or those "basketball" friends we mentioned above. Diversity in relationships, it has been said, is the spice of life, and I could not agree more. The world is such a small place now, with everyone having access to almost anyone else in the world via the cell phone that sits in our pocket. Welcoming opportunities to come in contact with and get to know people from different backgrounds, different religions, and different nationalities will not only enrich your life tremendously. It will also help the world in a "greater good" kind of way because you will be adding to the openness that our world offers to us instead of detracting from it.

Let me clarify that I am making a distinction between friends and associates. Friends are the people with whom you share a special bond and have connected with in a deep way. Associates are people you know and with whom you come in contact during the normal course of any given day, but may not be initially close to. And who knows, maybe these associates will become friends over time, which would also be fun!

DON'T BE A WORKHORSE

DIVERSITY WITH ASSOCIATES is very important because you don't want to become so isolated that you wear blinders with respect to your connections with other people. Back in the day, when horses pulled plows in the fields, farmers put blinders on those animals so they wouldn't be distracted from doing their work by any occurrences. The result was that, day after day after day, for its entire life, the horse never got to know anything more than its work, which is exactly what the owner of the horse wanted. Only when the horse was put in his stall for the night did the owner take the blinders off. Wow, now the horse got to take in all the events inside its twelve foot by ten foot stall. If it was lucky, the horse might even spy an aimless insect climbing up a wall of the stall. Sounds exciting, doesn't it? No, of course it doesn't. The insect might be most exciting and enjoyable to the horse because it never had the opportunity to know anything or anybody more exciting.

I don't want the most exciting thing in your life to be an insect on the wall either, and that is exactly what will happen (metaphorically, of course) if you become too isolated from other people.

Can you give me an example?

Take the All-American college football player who is destined to go pro upon graduation. What if the only friends or acquaintances he has besides his family are his coaches and his teammates? He is so sure about his career in football that he doesn't attend to his studies and they fall by the wayside. He doesn't diversify in his relationships or interests. So he graduates and is drafted right away into the best team in the National Football League. Let's just say for the purposes of this story, he's drafted by the Baltimore Ravens. One day, suddenly, our star breaks his leg or tears some ligaments in his knee beyond feasible repair while playing a pick-up game of basketball. End of football career.

Unfortunately, this athlete has nothing left because he'd focused so completely on football during his high school and college career. He doesn't know any thing other than football, nor does he know very many people who do. In other words, he is left down and out with no one to turn to. What a terrible and frustrating position to be in! And our star athlete probably can't obtain a sports announcer job either. He likely isn't experienced enough, or even well-versed enough to do that because he never paid much attention to his education while in school—he had such a singular focus, with extremely limited groups of friends and acquaintances. Yes, I'm generalizing here for the purposes of illustration, but I bet you get my point.

Anybody who has played or currently plays high school or collegiate sports has heard this type of story before. I am probably not telling you anything new here, but I want to reinforce that becoming too insular in your associations can be detrimental to you both now and in the future.

In summary, while it is in your best interest to have true close friends who share your same goals, aspirations, tastes, and interests, do not close your mind to anyone. Give everyone a chance to share what they know with you and, in return, freely share your knowledge and experiences with them. By doing so, you'll have the good fortune to hold on to a variety of people and relationships that will enrich your life now and in the years to come.

Here's a challenge to end this chapter: Write down what title/position/role you'd like to achieve one day. Now, go find someone currently in that position and meet them face-to-face.

START NOW!

What will YOU do as a result of reading this chapter?
YOUR Thoughts on Friends

CHAPTER THREE

MORE ON DIVERSITY

Not only is it important to be diverse in your associations with people, but it is important in every other aspect of your life as well. Don't tie yourself down to one type of music or one type of clothing or one type of job or one type of anything. At least not until you have given thought to all your other options. You need to be open-minded about things before making decisions. My parents said it best when they strongly suggested that I get to know many different girls before I attached myself to one of them. You see, they didn't want me to get married to someone only to discover, years into the marriage, that I had missed out by not dating other girls beforehand. This kind of discovery can obviously be detrimental to a relationship.

OK, OK, I'll be diverse. But why are you talking about marriage Jason? I'm sixteen years old or I'm twenty-two and I like the single life. I don't even want to think about marriage yet.

The point here isn't about marriage; the only reason I mentioned it is to illustrate my point about being open-minded and open to what the future may hold. If you don't begin to think about your future now, you won't have a future desirable enough to think about. When we talk about goals in chapter seven, this point should become even clearer to you.

Got it. Now, exactly how can this diversity deal help me out? Where does it fit in my life?

I have tried to follow the policy of diversity myself as closely as possible. For example, I have played just about every sport, ranging from football to golf to table tennis. So what, right? Let me explain why this is important.

The scenario is that you are a senior in college majoring in business, and you are being interviewed for a job by a distinguished company in your area. You have had many other interviews, but you really want this job with this particular company. Right from the start, the interview isn't going so well. You begin to get a little nervous. Your interviewer seems to be much too busy looking out the window and tapping her fingers on her desk to be paying any attention to you. To put it bluntly, the interview is going downhill fast and the chance of recovery is looking slim, to say the least. You start to sweat a little.

Looking for the quickest way out the door, you notice a Baltimore Orioles cap in the corner of the room. In a last-ditch attempt to engage the interviewer, you mention something about how one of the Orioles' pitchers has been doing lately. Suddenly, the interviewer is actually looking at you, paying attention. She begins to ramble on about the past few games and how the Orioles are doing this year in general, and before you know it, you two have talked about baseball for over thirty minutes. After the interview is over, you are invited to go to tomorrow night's game with the interviewer and her husband and, oh yeah, you got the job! Pretty neat, huh? And all because you knew a little bit about baseball.

Does this scenario sound like it could really happen? Let me tell you before you answer that it actually happened to a friend of mine just before he graduated from college. I could hardly believe it myself. The kicker to this story is that there were more than one hundred applicants for this particular job, many of them with arguably much better qualifications than my friend. True story.

I'll try to learn a little about sports, but I really don't like it all that much. Does that mean I'm out in the cold when it comes to this diversity business?

Of course not. Diversity does not just include sports. I want you to be as diverse as you can, in as many aspects of your life as possible. The world has so much to offer that it would be impossible to accomplish even .000001 percent of the things available to us, even if we lived to be a hundred and ten. My observation is that most successful people—defining success using their definition, not mine—have a variety of interests outside their main career focus.

OPEN-MINDEDNESS

I WOULD ALSO like you to understand that open-mindedness and diversity go hand in hand. In other words, you must be open-minded enough to try the many diverse options life has to offer.

A perfect example of a closed mind being opened wide happened one summer to a close friend's girlfriend. I was on vacation in North Carolina with my friend Ben and his family. Ben and I hunted together and we also enjoyed target shooting every once in a while. So we decided to load up the guns and the girlfriends and spend a nice afternoon with some target shooting. When we got to the shooting range, Ben's girlfriend decided she was afraid to shoot a gun. "Guns are just too dangerous for me," she said.

After about an hour or so of laid-back coaxing and gently explaining how fun and exhilarating target shooting was, we finally got her to take a shot. Suddenly, she found that she actually enjoyed the sport. From that moment on, she had twice the amount of turns as we had with the gun that day. All that needed to happen was for her to give it a try. Without that willingness to at least try, she would never have known that she actually really liked target shooting.

Another more recent example of the benefits of open-mindedness comes from one of our young adult editors, Paul, who had an opportunity to move to Maryland for a year for some job training with our coaching company. This was a bit unnerving for him; he was from Oregon on the West Coast, where he was born and had lived the entire twenty-two years of his life. Well, if truth be told, he was scared. Added to the mix was that Paul was getting married in Oregon and had to move to Maryland a week later, so this decision and the subsequent move needed to be navigated by him *and* his new bride, Renée. Moving across the country, away from his lifelong friends, family, and all things familiar to him for a full year job commitment was *way* out of his comfort and familiarity zone. But Paul and Renée took the risk anyway and moved east to Baltimore three days after their honeymoon, where they lived and worked for an entire year.

Today, Paul will tell you that even though the move was not easy and he did have moments when he missed his friends and family back in Oregon, the decision to make the move was one of the best decisions of his life. He and Renée were open-minded enough to make the move, even though they were not sure how it would work out. They made new friends, took weekend trips to places they would not have seen otherwise, and made memories they'd never forget. Paul now says that the best part of the whole experience for both him and Renée is that now, when they have decisions to make, even big ones, they view them with much more of an open mind than they would have had they not lived in Baltimore for that year. They have that experience to lean on, which has helped them navigate life in a much more enjoyable, freeing, and adventurous way.

All I ask is that you give it a try, whatever *it* is. After that, and only after that, you can form your own—informed—opinion. I don't want you to go through life ignorant of all the wonderful things the world has to offer.

I'd like to pause here to tell you about a free tool I helped to create that will help you understand your personal level of open-mindedness. Not only does this tool assess your open-mindedness, it also coaches you, through tips and tricks, to be more open-minded than you are today, if that is something you desire. It's called the Lizard Quiz. Go to www.lizardquiz.com, spend a few minutes answering twenty-eight simple questions, and voilà! You will get your personalized LQ (Lizard Quotient) and a robust report explaining both what your score means and the things you can do to improve how you engage diversity, new ideas, and change. I think you'll find it interesting and fun, but the question is: Will you be open-minded enough to take it? (See what I did there?)

Why is it called the "Lizard Quiz"?

The answer to that question is the topic of another book, *Still the Lizard*, by Steve Scanlon, which you'll want to read after this one if the journey to authentic sustainable change is something you're interested in.

NO SHUDDAS EITHER

I DON'T WANT you to suffer from a case of the shuddas either.

What the heck are the shuddas?

The shuddas occur when you look back and think to yourself, "Instead of doing what I did, I shudda done this" or "I shudda done that." Like when your alarm goes off in the morning and you think to yourself that you shudda gone to bed earlier the night before. You know the feeling.

One of my roommates during my freshman year at Loyola had a terrible case of the shuddas. He was a super gifted lacrosse player and without a doubt could have made the varsity lacrosse team. He, like many of us freshman, didn't quite have his priorities straight 100 percent of the time and ended up not even trying out for the team. Loyola had a great year and went on to play Syracuse for the national championship. Man, talk about a bad case of the shuddas! He said that if he had known ahead of time that Loyola would play in the national championships, he wudda made the effort to join the team.

It is said that hindsight is 20/20. He did learn from that experience, though. He tried out and made the team the following year and had a fun collegiate lacrosse career thereafter.

Oh yeah, shuddas and wuddas kinda go together.

Please don't go through life with a case of the shuddas or wuddas. Instead, go out and chase your dreams and wishes. Turning dreams into reality has been described by some as the true meaning of happiness. Do you want to be happy?

You may be suffering from a case of the wuddas or shuddas and not even know it. Many of us get so caught up in our day-to-day activities that we forget about the big picture of what we really want to do in life. A great way to find out if you are suffering from these afflictions is to think about the answers to the following questions.

If money were no object and you only had six months to live, would you be doing what you are presently doing with your life? Would you stay in New York City if you really wanted to move to Colorado? Would you continue to work or go to school where you do now? Would you have the same friends you now have? Would you continue spending time on unimportant day-to-day activities, or surfing the web or social media for three hours at a time if it meant sacrificing your main goals in life? If your answer to these questions is "no," you may indeed be suffering from a case of the wuddas or shuddas. And you may want to take a closer look at your life to get yourself motivated to do what you really want to be doing.

During the rewrite of this book in 2019, many of my young editors asked me to take a closer look at the above paragraph. They reminded me that many times, money can be a hindrance to getting what we desire out of life. They also wanted to make sure that you did not take the above suggestions too far, taking into account only the small picture of the here and now and ignoring the bigger picture purpose of your life.

I get it, and I appreciate that warning. And I will concur that much of life is a balance. If your *only* decision-making mode was "money is no object and six months to live," then sure, you may have moments of fleeting excitement (let's quit school and our jobs and max the credit cards taking a month-long trip around the world with all our best friends), but you would surely also experience deep levels of disappointment, regret, and possibly depression (sitting on the park bench with no job and no place to live because you weren't able to pay the rent due to your crazy trip around the world). My observation of thousands of successful people over the years is that the solution to this pendulum-swinging kind of thinking is to recognize that there are situations when it makes sense to ask yourself the "six months, money being no object" type of questions *and* there are times when it makes sense to think about the bigger picture of life and the story you ultimately want to write with that life of yours. It's yet another "both/and," not an "either/or" situation.

"BECAUSE IT'S THERE"

I'M SURE YOU'VE heard of people who enjoy climbing treacherous mountains: Mt. Everest in Nepal or Cerro Torre in Argentina. When many of these people are asked why they took on such ventures when they knew they could be killed during the effort, oftentimes they give an answer like, "Because it's there."

What? What in the world kind of answer is that?

You will personally never know or understand this kind of answer unless you go to the bottom of a mountain and start climbing. You will then either totally detest climbing mountains and figure that the people who do it "because it's there," must have an extreme, out-of-the-ordinary love of pain, or you will feel exhilarated by the experience of climbing and understand that these people see a challenge in the mountain and won't feel satisfied until they conquer it and all other mountains that happen to lay in their path of life. You may even find a different answer. My point is that you won't know *any* answers until you try it for yourself. Again, only then can you formulate your own opinion. You may not even care about the answer and don't think you want to go through the trouble of finding it, but you'll never really know unless you try it.

When I say that it would be beneficial for you to be as diverse in your life in as many ways as possible, I mean it with all the sincerity I can muster. You will learn, among other things, how to be nonjudgmental about people who are different from you.

One of our young American editors lived in Turkey, and she says that when she visited the States, she regularly heard comments about the people with whom she lived such as "Muslims are violent and they hate Americans." This appalled her as she knows these comments to be completely untrue. She lived among Muslim people for much of her life and knows them to be amazingly wonderful and caring people. These comments stem from thought processes that are detrimental to our understanding of the world in which we live. People fear what they don't know. I tell you this so your understanding and appreciation of the diversity of our world is broader and more well-rounded. Here's another one…

I had the opportunity to travel to the former Soviet Union during the summer of 1989 (of course, it wasn't "the former" then) for about three weeks. To fully understand the context of US/Soviet relations during that time in history, Google it, but let's just say that it was just before the fall of the Berlin Wall and things were a bit tenuous. During that trip, I learned things about the Soviet culture that many people in the US didn't then, and really still don't, know very much about. I met some of the nicest and most sincere people while I was there.

There was one evening in particular when a few of us in the group I was with were invited in for dinner with a Soviet family. We thought that dinner would last an hour or two and then we would come back to our hotel for the evening. Nope. Even though our dinner hosts didn't know more than ten words of English and no one in our group was well-versed in Russian, the evening went on for over four hours. It included some of the best food I've ever tasted and some of the deepest and most meaningful communication I've ever experienced.

Stories were acted out that night, laughter broke down any communication barrier that existed, and promises were made to keep in touch via letter by the end of the night. It concluded with long hugs and tears over the ending of an amazing night and the beginning of deep relationships.

When I returned home from this trip, I got a lot of negative feedback, statements such as, "They must have been pretty mean over there, being Russian and all." Or "The way they live is weird." I tried my best to explain that they were not weird at all—*different* from us, but certainly not weird. Yeah, sure, at that time in history they did live a very different lifestyle from the one most of us did in the West. But the point is, they were humans just like us in the US, and they deserved the same respect as everyone else. They were our neighbors in this thing called humanity. They just happened to live a little farther away from us than our neighbors next door. If close-minded people just widened their horizons, they would not make such foolish statements.

As author Liz Murray says, "We are all humans, the homeless person you see on the corner is just our homeless neighbor."

The more you do to get involved with life, the more you will begin to appreciate other people's jobs, lifestyles, cultures, habits, etc. That is because you'll not only know *what* others do, but *why* they do those things. So, please do not restrict yourself in any way when it comes to relating to people who are different from you or allowing yourself to experience what is unfamiliar.

Thanks for showing me that I need to do and be exposed to many things. I'm going to go out right now and join the track team and the debate team and do community service and buy a mountain bike and write a book and get my pilot's license and…

Needless to say, don't get so fired up that you try to do everything right now. Yes, the name of this book is indeed *Start Now*, but you also need to start smart. I don't want you to spread yourself too thin and suffer from competing commitments and desires to the point that you don't actually do anything. Please do not get yourself into more things at one time than you can handle, because then you will run the risk of losing sleep or rising blood pressure, and you may end up blaming it all on me. And I'm not really looking for that kind of pressure from you. I myself have bitten off and chewed too much at times and that is NOT fun at all. During those times, I found that I began to sacrifice certain important aspects of my life and ultimately, everything suffered. The key to avoiding that pain is to pace yourself with your diversity, wants, and desires. Just a word of caution here. But please do not let that caution get in the way of your getting involved with or learning about as much as you possibly can during your life. Don't let the world pass you by. Instead, chase after it, and be sure to smell the roses along the way too.

START NOW!

What will YOU do as a result of reading this chapter?
YOUR Thoughts on Diversity

CHAPTER FOUR

GOOD HUMAN RELATIONS

LET'S BEGIN THIS chapter with a list of ideas I saw one day at Loyola on the wall of my freshman academic adviser's office. The list was titled "The Ten Commandments of Good Human Relations."

1. Speak with people. There is nothing so nice as cheerful words of greeting.
2. Smile at people. It takes 72 muscles to frown, only 14 to smile.
3. Call people by name. The sweetest music to anyone's ears is the sound of his or her name.
4. Be friendly and helpful. If you want to have friends, be friendly.
5. Be sincerely cordial. Speak and act as if it were a genuine pleasure to serve people.
6. Be considerate of the feelings of others. No one likes to be rebuffed.
7. Be thoughtful of the opinion of others. There are three sides to a controversy—yours, the other person's and a reasonable middle ground.
8. Be genuinely interested in people. You can appreciate anyone if you just give it a try.
9. Be generous with praise and cautious with criticism.
10. Be alert to render a helpful service. Above all, what counts in life is what we do for others. Act as if you were the others.

My parents taught me, mostly by example, how to properly treat people. Their teaching went almost hand in hand with the above commandments and I tried my best to follow them while growing up and throughout my adult years. The older I get, the more important these simple rules seem to be. I know most of you have heard this before, but these commandments and my parents' teachings basically boil down to the Golden Rule: Treat people the same as you yourself would like to be treated and you will often be treated that way in return. But I'd like to take it even one step farther. I find that if I treat people *better* than I would ever wish to be treated, I get a pretty good feeling inside *and* I am "magically" treated absolutely fantastically in return.

I suppose I knew the basics of the Golden Rule all along. But it did not really dawn on me till the summer I first went down to Chipley, Florida, to learn about investing in real estate and discounted mortgages. Let me give you a bit of context here.

Before he retired, my father was a physician, but he also was, and still is, an active real estate investor. His real estate activities led him to attending workshops to educate himself on the finer points of the investing game. One of the workshop leaders who gave seminars around the country was a man named Jimmy Napier. Jimmy was a robust, very kind man who offered to anyone who would take him up on it a visit to him in his hometown, Chipley. While there, his visitors were welcome to shadow him for as long as they wanted, observing exactly how he went about the business of investing in real estate. When my father heard about this offer, he asked Jimmy if it would be all right to send his youngest son (that would be yours truly) down for a bit. Jimmy said sure, and that summer saw me driving solo the thousand miles from Maryland to Florida at age nineteen.

It took me a couple of days to make the drive, and when I got to the place on the map (remember, this was pre-GPS days) where Chipley was supposed to be, there was not much there that I could see besides a laundromat, a small gas station, and a Piggly Wiggly, which I had never even heard of. Turns out, by the way, that Piggly Wiggly was and still is one of the nation's largest grocery store chains. Back to my story—I showed up at the address I had written down for Jimmy's house. I was a bit travel worn and wide eyed and wondering what I had gotten myself into. I had grown up right outside of Washington, DC, and though I didn't realize it, was apparently *way* more of a city boy than I thought. Chipley, Florida, is as opposite a city as a town can get. Think lots of fields for farming—I mean, lots of them. Long stretches of one-lane roads with most driveways of the dirt variety. There wasn't much there at all—except the nicest people in the world.

Not only did I not know, I had never even spoken with anyone I would be spending that summer with. But when I got there, I was treated as though I had been a member of the Napier family for years. These people had no idea what I was like or how trustworthy I was or anything about me at all, but it didn't seem to matter to them. And in my turn, I couldn't help but be as friendly and cordial as I knew how. Mostly just to show my appreciation for their unselfish acceptance of me. I didn't even have to try to be nice either, really. It just came naturally as a response to them being super nice to me. One couldn't be anything but congenial to these people. It's almost as if I didn't have a choice. Thank you, Jimmy, Cricket, Judy, Debbie, Albert, and Luke for reinforcing that lesson to me and for the whole experience. I've never forgotten it.

Wouldn't it be great for others to think about you the way I thought about those amazing people in Chipley? It can happen and will indeed happen when you start following these human relations commandments, especially the Golden Rule one.

After some practice you will find that treating people like gold makes you feel so good inside that you will want to do it every time you come in contact with someone, even your adversaries! Yes, even the haters. I've heard it said that you should "kill 'em with kindness" when it comes to people you don't like that much. I say, "Just be kind." The nicer you are to the people you aren't really fond of, the fewer of these people you will have in your life. Psychologist Carl Rogers came up with the concept of Unconditional Positive Regard, or UPR. UPR is the basic acceptance and support of a person regardless of what the person says or does. I have experimented with this concept in a few different ways. There have been times when I've told myself that for the next twenty-four hours, no matter what the circumstances or what people say to or about me, or how well or poorly people engage me, I will practice regarding them positively. Again, no matter what. These experiments have been a bit harder for me than I would like to admit—especially when getting cut off in traffic, experiencing bad customer service from the cable company, or having acquaintances take extra advantage of our hospitality—all of which have happened during these twenty-four-experiments. But even though they have been difficult, they have also been way worth it; each of them has ultimately yielded my being more positively regarded by others than I had been before. Yet another example of getting in return what we put out there toward others.

TEN TIMES THE VALUE

I HAVE SEEN many times in action the old adage, "What goes around comes around," and as a result, I figure that if I am a person who gives unselfishly when it goes around, I'll probably be given abundantly when it comes back. I can tell you that during my adult life I have tried my darnedest to live by this adage and it just plain-old works (as exemplified by the UPR experiment above). It may not be perfect all the time, and there were a few instances I can point to when living out this adage has led me to be taken advantage of a bit here and there. But I'm OK with that and here's why: If the general direction of your life includes giving and receiving abundantly, and you must endure a knucklehead taking advantage of you along the way here and there, so be it. I still consider that a huge win. This life does not promise us that knuckleheads will not interfere from time to time. In fact, it's been my experience that the knuckleheads will be there no matter what. So I say let's give and receive with abundance. The alternative is to always be on the lookout to get what's "yours," and to expend a lot of energy trying to figure out how others are looking to take advantage of you. I've watched people approach life that way and it doesn't look like much fun. I'll take the general direction of abundance, thank you very much, and I hope you do too.

This idea even applies when you have had a particularly bad experience with someone. I would encourage you to keep "ten times the value" in mind, and to try to make amends with that person as soon as possible. You both will be better off, and you never know when you might need each other in the future. No burning bridges.

Sounds good, but give me a concrete example of exactly what you are talking about.

Sure! There was a time in the mid-1990s when Phil Bressler ran most of the Domino's Pizza franchises along the Mid-Atlantic coast. He had the practice of giving a dissatisfied customer ten times the value back to make amends for a rare mistake. In other words, if a pizza came to your house burned and he found out about it, he would make sure you got coupons for ten free pizzas—no questions asked. He felt people didn't need to be just satisfied, but rather *delighted.* In this manner he repaired bridges with his customers before they actually collapsed, and reinforced the infrastructure for their continued patronage of his stores. What a great practice! Those ten pizzas didn't cost all that much, especially compared to the business he would have lost had he not taken those proactive measures. Plus, he got to travel around the country proclaiming that he gave unhappy customers ten times the value of their dissatisfaction back. And that was in the '90s. With today's social media, something like this travels the socials like wildfire and creates a positive buzz that no ad ever could.

Here is another more recent example.

Nordstrom has a long and storied history of getting this human relations deal very right. In the midst of editing this book, one of our young adult editors, Jordan, went to a Nordstrom store to pick up a pair of shoes she had ordered online. When she opened the box in the store, she discovered that the shoes inside were not the ones she ordered. She needed the shoes she'd ordered for the coming weekend and they were not in stock in that store. The salesclerk went out of her way to have the correct shoes overnighted to Jordan for free *and* gave her coupons for four free meals in the Nordstrom Cafe, just because Jordan "was a patient customer and smiled at her." Wow!

OK fine, these are retail/commercial examples, but how does all this fit into my personal life?

I would like you to try to give ten times the value to the people with whom you come into contact throughout your day.

If this is a new idea for you, I suggest that you start small, but start now. A smile and a nice gesture will do the trick.

The smiles I get from people when I make the "ten times the value" effort is incredibly rewarding and makes me smile even more. For example, when I am at the checkout station at the grocery store or drug store, I am exceptionally friendly and outwardly appreciative of the checkout person's service. Clerks of every kind probably rarely get told what a great job they are doing, so they love to hear this feedback when it comes their way. Really, anyone would. It makes both of us feel good, and it's so easy. A win/win situation!

Try it out yourself. The next time you're checking out at a grocery or convenience store, smile and compliment the person at the register. Maybe it's the way they're dressed or their efficiency you notice, or the cleanliness of the store or a piece of their jewelry that catches your attention. You're just practicing at this point, so you can't mess up. The worst-case scenario is that they don't return the smile or the compliment. You both are in the same spot you would have been if you did not smile or say anything, so you really have nothing to lose. But the upside is great. I've gotten huge smiles back, laughter sometimes, and often a quick connection that would not have been made otherwise. Those connections can sometimes be the ten-times-the-value thing that can make a huge difference in someone's day—and yours. Here's another one: Compliment the next service person you come across on what a great job they're doing and see what happens. I think you will like the results.

This kind action may take a little concentration and effort at first if they have not been part of your regular deal, but after a while they can become second nature. People will start making mental note of your actions, and that mental note is the foundation of the reputation you are building for yourself. And your reputation is what will make you admired and sought after (or not), and most importantly, will create situations in which you can have a platform to add significant value to other peoples' lives.

These important human relationship skills will help you no matter what you want to do in life. No matter what profession or personal situation you choose, you will be in contact with other people. The better your interpersonal skills, the better off you will be: You'll move higher up the corporate and/or social ladder, people will come to you for help, you'll be in a better position to go to others for help, and others will respect your opinions and want to be in your company. More people are the heads of major organizations (teams, corporations, nonprofits, groups, etc.) not simply because they are intelligent, but rather because they possess excellent human relationship skills honed over a long time. And I get it that you may not have much of an interest in leading a big company one day, and that's cool, but these are the types of skills that will help you with whatever you choose to do in life.

In summary, just be nice to people and they will be nice back. After all, it *is* the Golden Rule.

START NOW!

What will YOU do as a result of reading this chapter?
YOUR Thoughts on Good Human Relationships

CHAPTER FIVE

NEGOTIATION

I've heard it said once or twice that no one gives you something for nothing except Mommy and Daddy. If that's the case, you must learn how to be an effective negotiator to get what you want in life. Negotiation is a skill that no one really ever perfects, but if you're good at it, you'll be able to get many things in life that you may not have otherwise. Negotiation is defined as the act of conferring with another person to settle a matter of mutual concern. Looking at it this way, you negotiate every day. At school, every time you speak up in class you are conferring with the teacher and class to settle some matter that may appear on an exam. When you go to a store, even the grocery store, you confer with the cashier to settle the matter of completing your purchase. When you go to a party or social event, you sometimes confer with someone who has caught your eye to settle the simple matter of whether you are interested in each other or not. Any of you who have worked in the business world certainly knows that every single day you must confer with others to settle some matter, urgent or otherwise.

Because we have established that we negotiate every day, it's probably a good idea to excel at this skill as much as we possibly can. The following pages will give you some insight on how to be a better negotiator.

Being a good negotiator will help you in working out a fair (and I'm sure deserving) curfew for yourself with your parents, discussing subjects with your teachers or professors as to why you might be unable to take an exam on time, buying consumer products (such as clothes, bicycles, electronics, etc.), working out a fair rate of pay with your boss, purchasing an automobile, and, of course, working on relationships with just about anybody.

Most of the techniques covered in this chapter will be helpful when you are the consumer, whether a consumer of clothes, cars, computers, or toys such as boats, skis, or whatever. I chose to emphasize consumer negotiation because young adults can be taken advantage of as consumers in our society. Salespeople treated me differently when I was a young adult. That isn't right, but it happens. I believe that as consumers, everyone should be treated equally. The following techniques should help even the playing field, if not tilt it in your favor a little.

Finally! I know I sometimes get taken advantage of as a young adult, but I never know what to do about it.

Good. Let's dive right in and see how we can learn to be better negotiators.

HELP OTHERS GET WHAT THEY WANT

First and foremost, you must realize that negotiation is a technique in which you are striving to get what you want, while at the same time striving to give the other person what he or she wants. As weird as it sounds, you should concentrate more on trying to give the other person what they want. Remember when I told you earlier that if you help enough people get what they want, you will surely get what you want? Well, this holds especially true in regard to negotiations.

During negotiations, especially at the outset, you should listen much more than you speak. This allows you to find out what the other person really wants. In terms of consumer products, it's usually money the other person wants, but if you listen hard enough (not just *hear* the other person, but really *listen* to them), you can find out *why* that person wants the money. Maybe then you'll be able to help him get what he really wants while at the same time saving yourself some money. For example, the main concern for a new saleswoman at a clothing store might be to build up a sizable client base. If you, the consumer, listen well, you may pick up on this and be able to work out a deal with her in which you agree to spread the word about what great service she provides if she gives you a discount on your purchases. You would be helping her get what she wants while at the same time getting what you want. This is called a win-win situation. Of course, we're assuming that she has the power to give discounts. If, for some reason, you can't figure out what the other person wants, just be blunt and ask, "What exactly is it that you want?" You may not always like the answer to this question, but you'll get one.

Jim Napier calls this listening technique "pacing" the other person. He says that you should listen at least twice as much as you speak—"After all, the good Lord gave us two ears and only one mouth." The more you listen, the more you will find out about the other person. This gives you a chance to learn about and understand the other person's personality and to make adjustments accordingly. The more you know about the other person, the more you can pace him and stay on top of where the negotiation is heading. You will learn what turns to take to help him get what you both want.

My friend, Andy, often negotiates with sellers to purchase used mobile homes. When he negotiates he rarely says anything, he just mumbles and nods his head. If he does speak, he beats around the bush so much that, in effect, he says something about nothing. He flusters the sellers so much with this technique that they think he is disappointed and sometimes end up improving their offer even before he opens his mouth! Only at the very end of the negotiating process, after he has an idea of where the seller is coming from and what he really wants, does he actually speak. In minutes, a deal is made or he is off to see another mobile home.

Andy's technique is very amusing to watch, but the main point of sharing it now is to teach you to *keep the other person talking*. The more they talk, the better you'll be able to figure out what they really want and, subsequently, you can try to satisfy both your needs. With a little practice, you'll find that it is possible and most favorable to do both. It also makes you feel good inside to know that you helped someone else get what he wants while at the same time getting what you want. And if you can't accomplish both, move on. However, it is best if both sides leave the negotiating table feeling like winners. If for some reason there can only be one winner, make sure it is the other side. You may suffer a short-term defeat, but in the long run you'll be much better off. Although you may not come out ahead in that particular situation, you won't have the reputation of coming out ahead in a situation where there is one winner and one loser.

A friend of mine says, "You can shear a sheep many a time, but you can only skin 'em once." In other words, you can negotiate with someone and have a win/win outcome many times, but as soon as you take advantage of a person, your dealings with him will be over forever. Makes a lot of sense, doesn't it? Again, the person to whom I'm trying to give the edge is you, but this edge should never emerge at the expense of someone else.

IT'S ONLY A GAME

THE SECOND THING you must realize is that negotiation is both a game and an art. It's an art because, as I mentioned before, people possess the ability for it in varying degrees, and if you practice, you can get better at it.

I personally view negotiation as fun and take part in it whenever I can. In fact, I would even go out to used car dealerships every once in a while to shop for a car, just to take part in some good-natured, heated negotiations. When I did it, I wasn't necessarily planning to purchase a car, though I was always open to that outcome. But it was a lot of fun to deal with the salespeople, who pride themselves on being professional negotiators. And, of course, they're very good. When I went, I expressed longstanding interest in a particular car, as if I were finally ready to purchase. You don't want to always act very interested while negotiating, and I'll tell you why in a bit, but the more serious I was, the more intriguing the negotiations were. I went all out, down to the test drive and even batting a purchase price back and forth.

This is a great exercise for you to try. When you go to purchase a car (motorcycle, boat, whatever) don't just go to one place. Plan to go to at least three or four, so you can practice negotiating.

When you go out, try to dress, look, and act as mature as possible. The only reason I suggest this is because the salesperson will take you more seriously if he thinks you are a young adult instead of a kid. You may be a little scared at first, but that's OK. Go through with it anyway. It's a great learning experience. If you don't do very well the first time, don't worry. Most of these salespeople are excellent at what they do and know how to make a consumer, especially a young consumer, feel uneasy and unsure. If this happens to you, just laugh it off; you're just practicing anyway. And if things get really bad, thank the salesperson for his time and simply walk away. Stay courteous, but remember that you don't owe the salesperson anything beyond that. Negotiation is a game and you're a player trying to have fun.

Jason, this is probably the best practice when trying to assimilate negotiating skills, but is it ethical?

Some might say that intentionally planning a few practice negotiations before your purchase may be wasting the salesperson's time. But you want to be sure you understand how to recognize the salesperson's tactics, and you are, in fact, in the market for a car. You can never have enough practice negotiating, and I do believe this to be a healthy and ethical means of practicing negotiating skills.

Thanks. I understand most of this preliminary stuff, now let me in on the guts of this material.

BE COOL

BEFORE YOU NEGOTIATE anything, you must remember to get in a laid-back frame of mind. Almost a "hey man, whatever happens, happens" frame of mind. At least you must sound as if you are in this mindset, even if, on the inside, you feel as if your life depends on the outcome of your negotiations. Let me explain. First of all, a relaxed attitude relaxes you and frees up your mind so you can think clearly. Secondly, it helps you to be a "don't-wanter."

What's a "don't-wanter"?

A don't-wanter acts as if he doesn't *really* want what is being negotiated, as if he can comfortably walk away from any deal no matter how far the negotiation has progressed. This is why I said earlier that you don't want to seem too interested in what you are negotiating for. If the other person sees that you are indifferent to what he has to offer, he may sweeten the deal a little to entice you into buying. You should practice a "be cool" attitude even when you really want what you are negotiating for.

I decided to try this out when I was seventeen and looking to purchase a boat. I was looking for a used ski boat in good shape for around six or seven thousand dollars. One of my brothers had agreed to split the cost and ownership with me. I studied up on ski boats and shopped around for months until one day I ran into a dream. I drove way out to Vienna, Virginia, from where I lived in Hyattsville, Maryland, to price a boat someone was selling. The seller wasn't there, but his mother took me around to the back of their house to see the boat. I was confronted with something that kinda, sorta resembled a boat, but that was covered with an old, ugly, green, dusty, cover-like thing. Minute by minute, I got more disappointed that I had driven so far from home on a Saturday when I could have been hanging out with my friends instead. But the owner's mother and I pulled off the cover, and when the dust settled, there sat my dream boat. It was exactly what I was looking for. The color was deep, dark blue, the same tone as the summer sky right before a monstrous thunderstorm. And it had splendid silver metal flakes glittering in the sun, so much so that it was almost blinding to the eye. It was a sixteen-foot-long Baja with a 115 horsepower Mercury engine. That means it was extremely fast—like a rocket on water! In short, this boat was the coolest thing I had come across in my life, and I wanted to pay his mother for "my baby" right then and there and take this beauty home with me, where it belonged. But instead, I swallowed hard and told his mother that it wasn't exactly what I was looking for, but maybe her son could call me about it when he came home, just to talk about it anyway. Understand now, it hurt me badly—I mean *badly*—to stall, because I was severely worried that someone else would come along that day and buy "my" boat out from under me.

That night the seller called and told me that he was asking $7,500 for the boat. I knew from my studies that was a fair price for that particular boat. But I explained to him that I wasn't really interested, especially at that price, but if he had time, I wouldn't mind taking the boat for a spin sometime. I don't know why, but he then told me that he hadn't had much luck selling the boat and he was getting ready to move out of town soon. As soon as he told me that, I knew he was a desperate seller, a "wanter," and so far I had been acting like a good don't-wanter. After about a week of negotiations and an exciting boat ride, I ended up purchasing it from him for $6,500, and that included some ski equipment I'll tell you about later.

That sounds pretty neat, but it also sounds a little too good to be true. Explain a little more about what happened.

Let's examine what took place here. First, I played the don't-wanter to a tee. Fortunately, to the seller I was just another person who didn't seem to be all that interested his boat. He expressed his frustration that he wasn't having much luck selling it, and that he was moving soon. By listening to his problems, I figured out a way to solve them by taking the boat off his hands in a timely fashion, while at the same time getting a heck of a price on my dream boat! A win-win situation.

Understand that such situations don't always turn out so perfectly, but if you're persistent enough, you will run across your fair share of them that do. I have since experienced not-so-successful negotiations, and I just chalk them up as learning experiences. After each experience I learn, and then am able to avoid, yet another negotiating technique that doesn't work so well for me.

Learn to be a don't-wanter now that you know what one is. This allows you to remove your emotions from negotiating. Salespeople often try to play on the emotions of young adults because, quite frankly, it's a very powerful trick in the salesperson's toolbox. Emotions can sometimes ruin any chance of your getting a good deal. One way to practice being a don't-wanter is to practice negotiating when you are not really invested in the outcome. In other words, when you aren't too attached to the idea of the item you're negotiating over. If you can practice with things you don't really want, you'll be in great shape when you're negotiating for something you actually do want.

PERSONALITY

Everyone has their own unique personality. An excellent skill that will take you far in life and in the negotiation process is the ability to size up and observe different personalities and adapt to them accordingly. The importance of this skill is impossible to overstate. People are much more comfortable when they feel that you understand their situation because it makes you seem just like them. This understanding becomes the on-ramp to a place of trust, and once trust becomes a part of the negotiations, the odds are that both parties will emerge winners.

This is another area where the more diversified you are, the better your skills become. Open-mindedness also plays an important role here. I have seen many people miss out on deals simply because they can't, or don't want to, deal with people who are different from them, even if those people have something they want. To me, that is foolishness.

My parents taught me to be myself, and to be proud of who I am and where I come from no matter what. By no means am I asking you to be someone you are not. At the same time, I don't want you to let your pride get in the way of the opportunities life throws you.

For example, if you are extroverted and find yourself negotiating with someone who seems to be introverted, realize it and act accordingly. Don't overpower this person and scare him away. Also, deal with the opposite gender as well as you deal with your own. Learn how to act around the "upper crust" of society as well as with those less fortunate. Different situations call for different behavior, and if you act accordingly, your negotiating efforts will go much further than if you don't.

ASK, ASK, AND ASK SOME MORE

While you're negotiating, you should constantly ask questions. But more importantly, you should always ask for more than you really want. There are two reasons for doing this. The first is that you may actually get what you're asking for, and the second is that if you ask for more than you want and you wind up finally compromising, you may still get what you originally wanted anyway. Asking for more allows you to make concessions that don't matter to you.

At the end of the week-long negotiation for my boat (lovingly named *Stealth*), as I wrote the check to pay for it,

I paused and told the seller that I was under the impression that his ski equipment came with the boat. I asked him if my impression was correct. He paused for a very long time and finally said that yes, my impression was indeed correct. I'm pretty sure he planned to keep the equipment for himself, but because I asked, I got it. Altogether, the equipment was probably worth about $400. Not bad.

All you have to do is ask. The answer may be no, but you certainly will never know if you don't ask. In his seminars, Jimmy Napier teaches that during a negotiation you must ask, ask, ask, ask, ask, and then ask some more to get what you want and to make sure you know exactly what is going on throughout the negotiation.

Some teachers go so far as to teach their students to never make a statement while negotiating. Instead, just ask questions, and even respond to a question with another question! It takes a lot of practice to be able to do this tactfully, but if done correctly, it can be very effective.

Remember that one reason you are asking these questions is to get the most you can out of the deal. But even more importantly, you are also concentrating on giving the other person what they want. I want you to get as much as you can out of the deal without stripping the other person completely. So make a good deal for yourself, but don't rob anybody blind in the process.

ALWAYS FLINCH AT, AND NEVER TAKE, THE FIRST OFFER

No matter what the other person's first offer is while you're negotiating, even if it's agreeable to you, flinch at it right away. You want to seem very surprised at the price or offer.

Whenever someone gives you an offer, he will watch intently for your first reaction. If you automatically flinch, you will throw him off and sometimes make him rethink and lower his offer even before you have the chance to say anything. I say automatically because you should make it an instinctive reaction even if the first offer is agreeable to you. Often, you will be given a chance at a better price or more favorable terms or extras. You could even have fun with this: Make the flinch very obvious and act as if it really hurts you to hear the price, almost as though you're wincing with pain. Try flinching in front of a mirror or a friend. It sounds corny, but it sure is effective. Let's be real. We're both, buyer and seller, trying to get the best price, and injecting a little humor into the mix can break through any confrontational tone in the negotiation to make it more relational for both parties.

Imagine that you are selling a lawn mower. When a potential buyer asks you the price and you answer, he flinches, as if he has just felt a sharp pain in his back. How would you feel? Probably fairly guilty, and to ease both your guilt and his pain, you may lower your asking price. Flinching might sound silly, but most of the time this technique works like a charm. It also allows you to back away from the first offer, which, as a rule of thumb, you should never, *ever* take. The reasoning behind this is that no matter what the situation, the deal can always be sweetened. Usually the seller starts high and doesn't really plan on getting his asking price anyway, so you shouldn't plan on giving it to him.

BE SMART... *AND* DUMB

Knowledge is power and information is one of the keys to success. History has proved this to be true time and time again. Evidence for it can be found in just about every war ever fought. The side who possesses the most information about the other side almost always emerges victorious. The more you know about the subject of your negotiation, and with whom you are negotiating, the better chance you have of emerging victorious as well. In the case of consumer products, information gathering is very easy via the Google machine. And if you start asking and calling around about the product in which you're interested, you'll find that for the most part, people will be more than willing to provide you with information and opinions.

OK, so now we know that information is key. Exactly what do we do with that information?

The answer is to keep all information in your head and don't let it come out of your mouth unless necessary. In other words, be smart *and* dumb. If you don't put your knowledge out on the table, you will find that the person with whom you are negotiating will sometimes go out of his way to help you understand a point, if for no other reason than that he feels sorry for you. This helpfulness can also overflow into the negotiations as well, which does wonders. Instead of the competitive spirit that usually gives negotiations a "you against them" tone, you can have the other person actually considering your needs and wants. This is the most ideal situation for you. The other person is trying to help you and, as we said before, you are trying to help him. Only a win-win situation can result.

Another technique that goes along with this is to never give yourself total authority, or at least never let the other person think you have it. Then you will always have a way out of a situation that you may not otherwise be able to handle. If you get in a position that is uncomfortable, you can always say, "I'll have to check with my partner on that," or "I don't think my parents will go for that." These statements instantly ease the pressure from you, even if you don't really have to check with anyone.

You'll find that used-car salesmen are masters at this technique. As soon as you give them your first offer, they instantly say that they have to confer with their manager. Then they go in some back room and supposedly talk over your offer with a higher authority. Whether they do or not I don't really know, but I do recognize and applaud their techniques.

However, you must remember that in gathering this all-important information, you must work in an environment that is based on honesty and integrity and free of suspicion and mistrust. If you break this rule, you can kiss your chances of getting what you want out of your negotiations—and life, for that matter—goodbye. Information is definitely the key to success, but if you do anything underhanded to get it, you will not succeed, at least not in the long run. Being both smart *and* dumb is part of the game of negotiating; lying, on the other hand, is deceptive and inexcusable.

TIME

Your time is the most precious possession you will ever have. God only gives us so much time to utilize on this earth, and we therefore need to use time wisely. There are many things in this world that, if wasted, can be replenished, but once you use time—wisely or not—you can never get it back, ever. And there's nothing we can do about that. So please, learn to respect time and not waste it.

One way to avoid wasting time is to understand the 80/20 rule. With regard to time and negotiating, the rule states that

80 percent of concessions occur in the last 20 percent of the time available to negotiate. Understanding this rule can help us out in two ways. First, it tells us that we should ask for more than we actually want so when we do make concessions at the end of the negotiation, we really don't lose.

The other lesson to be learned from the 80/20 rule is that the shorter we make the negotiation, the fewer concessions we have to make, simply because there is less time to make them. So how do we make the negotiation short? Jim Napier has a simple strategy to accomplish this. Once he understands what the other party has to offer, he makes a statement something like:

"Now that we understand each other, to save us both a bunch of time, why don't you just—I mean, so we don't have to dicker and bicker back and forth and all—why don't you just give me your bottom, and I mean *bottom* offer. Once you give me your price, that'll be it—no bad feelings—and either I take it or I leave it. Now, buddy, just give me the absolute bottom price you will take right here and now."

This statement usually cuts the negotiating time down to about five minutes or less. After he makes his statement and the other party makes his offer, Jim either takes it or leaves it, and the deal is either consummated or ended. I have seen him successfully use this technique while negotiating for everything from getting his lawn mowed by his grandson to negotiating hundreds of thousands of dollars' worth of real estate. The 80/20 technique isn't always suitable, and a milder form may work better for you. The point is to make the negotiation as short as possible so you won't have to give up much.

Don't let the other party put any time pressure on you. Instead, you put it on them. It doesn't matter whether you're the buyer or the seller. Many sellers will give you an offer on Wednesday and tell you that it is only good until Saturday.

This automatically puts you at a disadvantage, which is what it is meant to do. Don't accept the pressure; instead, put the time pressure on *them* by making your offer good for only so long. This stops the seller from continuously looking for the best offer and puts the pressure on him to sell to you while he has the chance.

Of course, this doesn't work in every situation. I mean, if you walked into a clothing store on Monday and it has 200 white polo shirts for $25 each, and you offer the salesperson $20 for one and tell him that your offer is only good until Wednesday, he would probably laugh right in your face. But maybe one of the other techniques mentioned in this chapter (such as ask, ask, ask or flinching at the first offer) would get you that shirt for $15. Remember, find out what the salesperson really wants.

Always be aware of the role that time plays in your negotiation. For example, there are situations where the more time someone spends with you trying to work out a deal, the more anxious he will be to close it. I have seen this many times in the mortgage banking business. Sometimes, the longer a loan officer spends trying to bring a loan together, the more anxious he gets to close it, and the more willing he is to compromise than he normally would be, just to get the loan out of the way. In other words, the loan officer would make exceptions to avoid being tied up in the deal any longer.

If you have the time and the patience, try this method on something you're about to purchase. Simply take up as much of the salesperson's time as you possibly can and see if, after a while, he doesn't give you a good deal just to get you out of his hair.

Also, be aware of other time constraints that might hinder negotiations with the other person. Is she moving in the near future, or does he need the money soon for something else?

Is the store about to close for the day? These are all time elements that, if you prepare for properly, you might be able to use to your advantage. Always be aware of what's going on around you.

LAST FEW THOUGHTS

After a little practice, you will learn what works for you and what doesn't, and you will quickly develop your own negotiating strategies, hopefully incorporating some of the ones I have just shared with you.

I should note, although you probably have already figured it out, that not all of these techniques necessarily go together. Certain techniques only work in certain situations. However, after you try them a few times, you'll begin to figure out which techniques work for you, when they work, and when they don't. I would like to leave you with just a couple more hints to keep in the back of your mind while you're learning how to negotiate.

1. **Expect a lot of nos.** Even pro negotiators hear nos on a regular basis. The difference between them and unsuccessful negotiators is that the pros deal with those nos professionally, then quickly move on. Look at it this way: The yes you're looking for resides in the land of no. One disadvantage you have as a young adult, compared to older people, is that others are much more apt to say no to someone your age. Don't dwell on that no as a whiner would; instead, thank the person for giving you the opportunity of receiving a no, because now you are that much closer to a yes. Not only will it surprise that person, but it's fun to do, as long as you possess the lighthearted approach

you're supposed to have while negotiating. All I'm really saying here is that you should realize nos are inevitable, and you should be prepared to deal with them.

2. ***All* fees are *always* negotiable.** This thought is pretty straightforward; please remember it. Terms like "firm," "nonnegotiable," "fixed," "solid," and "steadfast" are just used as negotiation tactics. These words don't mean much to those of us who are going to flinch at and negotiate the price down anyway. Even if the price is written down and looks official, don't sweat it; no matter what, the price or fee is always flexible and negotiable. And know this: The bigger the purchase, the more negotiable the price and any associated fees are.

3. **Don't lie.** Sometimes it's easy to lie while negotiating. You get caught up in trying to sell your bike for the highest price and the next thing you know, you're lying about how long you have owned it or exactly what shape it's in. Don't do it. Lying can be an addiction; once you start, it's very hard to stop because you have to start telling new lies to cover up your old ones, and so on, and so on. You will soon lose your credibility, which, in turn, will ruin your chances of completing many successful negotiations.

   By no means does this mean that you have to tell the whole truth from the outset, though. To tell someone how much you really want what he has, or to tell him that the only reason you aren't talking very much is because you are trying out a new negotiating technique you just learned, would be shooting yourself in the foot. I hope you can see the distinction. Don't ever lie in a negotiation, but don't necessarily offer information that isn't asked for either. If you have owned and abused the bike for five straight years, but the buyer doesn't ask how long you've owned it or how you've treated it, I don't see that you have any obligation to tell him, as long as you sell the bike "as is." This philosophy of telling the truth while negotiating has worked very well for me so far. I'm sure it will for you as well.

4. **Help others get what they want.** I started off the chapter with this thought, and I would like to end it this way as well. Just remember, if you help enough others get what they want out of the negotiating process, you will surely get what you want in return.

START NOW!

What will YOU do as a result of reading this chapter?
YOUR Thoughts on Negotiation

SECTION TWO:

HOW WE ENGAGE OURSELVES

CHAPTER SIX

K.I.S.S.

K.I.S.S. STANDS FOR Keep It Simple, Stupid.

I first learned this acronym and what it meant from my high school chemistry teacher, Mr. Roberts. To solve some of our chemistry problems, we had to use equations that were part of formulas that seemed to go on forever. If we tried to take on a whole formula at once to solve a problem, we would invariably become lost and end up coming up with the wrong answer. Then Mr. Roberts suggested that we try using the K.I.S.S. method to solve the problems.

This so-called "kiss" method sounded a little weird to us at first. But after some explanation and a little persistence from the teacher, we gave it a try. Instead of attempting to solve the problem as a whole, Mr. Roberts suggested we break it up into smaller parts. Solve each part separately and then, only at the very end, put all the parts back together to solve the bigger problem. It is such a simple and easy idea to execute. Like, really easy. After discovering the K.I.S.S. method, I found that the formulas were not really that difficult after all. I couldn't imagine successfully completing some of the problems until I learned to keep it simple. It's what got me through that class, and many other classes and work projects since.

The next time you must take on a major project that looks tough to accomplish as a whole, try breaking it up into parts to make it easier for yourself. For example, when you have an "impossible" twenty-page research paper to do for your history class (for all you high school students, yes, there are twenty-page papers due in college), simply break it into its parts. If you try to do it all at once (getting ready, choosing the topic, the research, the interviews, the outline, the writing, the editing, the notations, the cover, the summary, and so on), you'll invariably become frustrated.

Instead, if you break all the above pieces into separate, simpler parts, scheduling out each one into the time frame allotted for writing the paper, things will work out *much* better. It is very important to do each one of these parts on different days; otherwise, you might be defeating the purpose of dividing it into parts to begin with. Now that the paper has been divided into its simplest parts, it will seem like a piece of cake instead of that "impossible" project. In fact, just skip the "getting ready" part above and get to work. Remember the name of this book and read on.

Procrastination can often be the enemy of progress. If you put off doing something challenging until the last minute, you won't have the luxury of using the K.I.S.S. method. You will instead have to do your whole project at once and won't perform as well as you might have because you had to rush the job. So please do not procrastinate. If you start with the seeds of procrastination now by putting off writing a paper until the night before it is due, by the time you graduate from high school/college, the things that you will be putting off will have grown into bigger and more consequential items. As an adult, you risk your procrastination leading to your being known as a person who is not reliable and who doesn't get things done on time and/or correctly.

DON'T BE THAT PERSON!

Think about anything in your life that you have been taught how to do. You were surely taught by a teacher who used the K.I.S.S. method whether they, or you, knew it. Remember when you were first taught how to spell? If you couldn't figure out how to spell a long word like "understanding," your teacher suggested that you break the word up into syllables. Instead of having to spell the whole word at once, you would only have to spell a few short sounds that, when put together, would spell the longer word.

All sports coaches will tell you that the key to any sport is learning the basics. For example, you don't learn how to play basketball in a couple of hours. You are first introduced to the ball, then taught how to dribble, then how to shoot, then how to play defense, and so on. In other words, to learn the sport, it's broken down into its most basic components. Only when you have a grasp of the basics are the individual skills combined to make the game of basketball in its entirety.

This method makes the learning process a lot easier and can also make the improvement process run smoothly. If you are currently playing a sport and find your game lacking, simply break the game down to its most elementary parts to try to figure out exactly where you need work. Once the problem area is pinpointed, it can easily be singled out and worked on for improvement. That works much better than getting angry with yourself because you are not playing as well as you would like.

By now, you should see how breaking down difficult projects to their simplest parts makes them seem not so difficult after all. When you feel overwhelmed (and don't we all have that feeling from time to time?), don't forget to use the K.I.S.S. method to make it easier for yourself.

This idea has now proved so useful for my entire life and that of my clients that it made it became one of the six core values at our company, Rewire. Everything we do at our company goes through the filter of keeping it simple. If an idea or project or process cannot be readily understood or followed, we break it down even more. There have been several times throughout the company's history when this value has saved us a ton of time, frustration, and energy.

If this particular topic resonates with you, know that there is much that has been written/taught/thought about in recent years on simplicity, lean startups, minimum viable products, and the like. A quick internet search can provide you with plenty more information.

Notice that this is one of the shortest chapters in the book? Just tryin' to keep it simple!

START NOW!

What will YOU do as a result of reading this chapter?
YOUR Thoughts on Keeping It Simple

CHAPTER SEVEN

GOALS

You ABSOLUTELY, 100 percent must have goals!

The earlier you learn how to create and strive toward your goals and dreams in life, the more fulfilling and meaningful your life will be. Take a few minutes right now to jot down your first thoughts and the goals that come to mind while you're reading this chapter. Grab your favorite journal for this purpose, and keep it close by as you read through what's ahead. Usually, these will be the things you deeply desire in life but have never given enough thought to, to actually act on those desires. By writing down these thoughts, not only will you begin the process of imprinting them on your brain, but you also will have something tangible to look back to when you're finished reading this chapter.

If we don't have anything to strive for in our lives, we risk becoming stagnant and can quickly get stuck in a crappy rut for the rest of our lives. I've observed so many people who lack direction in their lives simply because they don't have any goals to keep them yearning and striving and moving forward. Some are aware that they are in a rut but don't know how to get out.

Creating and striving toward goals is the answer!

Let's start off with a little story that exemplifies the importance of goals in your life. During my freshman year in high school, I tried out for the soccer team. The first week of tryouts, the team played on a couple of different fields because the coaches weren't sure where the team was going to end up practicing for the rest of the year. The first couple of days, when we arrived at whatever field we were using that day, most of us would play a quick game of pick-up soccer to warm up before the coaches arrived. On the third day, we again arrived a little early to get in our warm-up game. We picked teams quickly and walked out onto the field, where we noticed that there weren't any goals set up. We were disappointed, but we walked back to the sideline and sat down on the bleachers and patiently waited until our coaches came. When the coaches got there, they asked us why we weren't on the field, warming up as we had done for the past two days. We pointed to the field and answered that we couldn't play soccer without any goals. The head coach pointed us to another field that did have goals, so we could start a proper practice.

Can you play the game of soccer without any goals?

Can you hit a target if you don't have one?

Can you play the game of life without any goals?

You see where I'm going here?

You must have goals!

J. C. Penney once said, "Give me a stock clerk with a dream, and I'll give you a man who will make history, but if you give me a man without a dream, I'll give you a stock clerk."

You must have goals!

TEN STEPS TOWARD YOUR GOAL

There are ten steps you must take to make sure you actually reach the goals you create for yourself. If you perform these ten steps, you will significantly stack the deck in favor of you reaching your goals. Think of them as secrets that hardly anyone else your age knows.

I like the sound of this so far, but why are you calling them secrets?

Because most people just don't know them, and of those that do, many don't actually follow them. These secrets are the keys that open the doors to your goals. They are what make your dreams come true. This is exactly the type of information that will give you an edge and allow you to enjoy life to the fullest.

Here are the ten steps to goal attainment:

1) Put yourself in a positive mindset.

Without this first step, it is difficult to accomplish anything in life. Thinking positively allows you to accomplish what you set out to do in life; thinking negatively doesn't. It's that simple.

You'll need this upbeat frame of mind throughout the rest of the steps. This first step is simple, but it's ever so important because without it, you won't get started, and starting something is getting it half done. It's the very reason for the title of this book. Always remember, a journey of a thousand miles begins with the first step.

During the rewrite of this book, one of our young adult editors made this comment after reading step one: "This is step one, which it should be because to accomplish most things in life, you have to be OK with things not going perfect. You have to accept that things will get messed up, go wrong, be messy, but you *have* to be positive about it to move forward and keep trucking!"

Another one of our editors had this to say about it: "This step is simple, but not always easy. With everything that comes at us throughout each day, a positive attitude can often be something that is difficult to sustain. When challenges are thrown your way, the first step to success is perceiving it in a manner that will allow you to excel, not be crippled by actions outside your control. Leverage only what you *can* control—a positive mental attitude being that first point of leverage."

I regularly get questions about *how* to do this first step. Sometimes it's not just as easy as "boom—there, I'm in a positive mindset, let's move on to step two."

There are times when you may just not be feeling it, and I get that. There are thousands of things to do and ways to get yourself in a positive mindset, but I'm going to give you two magic bullets that have worked for me and that I've seen work over and over and over again with others: physical movement and practicing gratefulness.

When you're moving your body—any type of exercise will do, even a walk around the block—the endorphins and forward thinking/creative chemicals in your brain are firing in such a way that the positivity flows naturally. Combine body movement with any type of gratefulness exercise (write down five things you're grateful for, tell someone you appreciate them, write someone a handwritten note, etc.) and you'll end up with a positive mental mindset.

2) Think about what you want in life and write it down.

This can be the most difficult step. That's because at this point in your life, you may have little to no idea what you want. Or, what you wanted last week isn't what you want right now. That's fairly normal for young adults, and this chapter should help ease some of that difficulty. You don't necessarily have to come up with a major, long-term goal, such as what you would like your occupation to be in ten years. For some of you, this long-term type of deal is possible, but for others, it may be more realistic to make a short-term goal, like "I want to get an A in English class this semester," or "I want to make the team this year."

If you're having any hesitancy at this point, start out with an even narrower, shorter-term goal, such as "I want to get an A on my next paper or test in English," or "I want to practice to make the team, every day for the next two weeks."

Whatever you decide to write down has to be very specific—as-specific-as-you-have-the-ability-to-be kind of specific. In other words, writing down "I want to lose weight" is not good enough. This statement is much too broad. If you wrote that down and then lost one pound, have you reached your goal? I wouldn't know, and neither would you. Arguably, you have reached your goal because you stated that you wanted to lose weight, and you did just that. But what if you're ten pounds overweight? Your goal has to be stated in specific, definite, and measurable terms, so that while you're striving for it, you can gauge your progress. Once you reach your goal, you will know it and be able to celebrate your success. Our example would be better stated by writing down "I want to lose ten pounds." That way, when you have shed your tenth pound, you will be able to relish the fact that you have attained your goal.

3) Identify *why* you want what you want in life.

What value does your goal provide for you? Why are you striving toward it? Is it really worth it to you? When you reach your goal, what will you have that you don't have now? These questions should all be answered specifically and positively. If any of them are answered in the negative, your motive behind your goal may need to be revised.

This step three is unequivocally the most important one in this goal setting/goal getting process, so please, I beg you, do not sleep on it. In fact, before moving on to step four, go back and reread the first paragraph of this step, answering each question until you feel confident and satisfied with your answers.

4) Write down a specific date by which you expect to reach your goal.

It will be more concrete because you are telling yourself that you really want to accomplish your goal by setting a time limit on it. It's no longer some far-off thought you once had, but something that will actually be fulfilled by the date you set. So, now you would state your weight loss goal something like, "I want to lose ten pounds by graduation, which is June 1."

5) Identify and educate yourself as to what you have to know to reach your goal.

Without this step, you may get into more than you can handle without realizing it. For example, having the goal to become a medical doctor is great, but if you're no good at or don't like science very much, it's probably an unrealistic and unreasonable goal for you. Some goals require vast amounts of knowhow, while others don't require much specialized knowledge at all. Whatever the case, once you have identified what you need to know, you will be able to put your goal in perspective as to its attainability for you, in your situation, with your gifts and talents. If you don't think you can learn all you need to know to reach your goal, or don't want to, this is the step where you can revise your goal to something that is better suited to your learning level and desires.

For your goal of losing ten pounds, you should learn as much about nutrition as possible and how the body reacts when it is going through a weight-loss program. You should also plan ahead of time if you are going to exercise, and if you are, exactly how, when, and where. Some time on Google or a trip to the library or a doctor can help take care of this step. You can also find some apps to download to help you along your way, many of which may also provide you with an online community to help cheer you along and offer advice/tips.

6) List the obstacles you will have to surmount to reach your goal.

If the goal is worthwhile in your life, obstacles are bound to get in your way along the way. Instead of being surprised by them, or suffering major setback when they occur, you will expect and can more easily overcome them. Instead of getting a surprise punch to the face by these obstacles, you will have time to prepare for and maybe even be able to duck it altogether because you did a little planning ahead of time. An ounce of prevention is worth a pound of cure, right?

Some of the obstacles you might have to overcome with your weight loss goal might be cravings to eat at odd times, at parties and other social settings, during holidays (because food seems to be a big part of every holiday), peer pressure from family or friends to eat when we shouldn't, or maybe when your favorite junk food presents itself. By listing these obstacles, you will be better prepared to clear these hurdles when they get in your way.

7) List the people and/or groups you must work with or get support from to reach your goal.

No matter what we do in life, we must engage with others to do it. This step involves more planning that will allow you to eliminate most of the unexpected. For instance, you are going to be in constant contact with your family and friends while you are on your weight-loss journey. Plan to communicate your goal with them, so they can encourage you and cheer you on in your effort to lose ten pounds by June 1. You may end up telling everyone about this goal, but you will most likely have to work with your family and friends to complete it. If you had to lose more than ten pounds, maybe you would plan to join a weight loss program such as Weight Watchers or engage a health coach. But for ten pounds, your family and friends may do just fine.

8) Develop a game plan.

With this step, you will start to wrap up your goal-setting strategy and put it all together in one clean package. Using steps one through seven, create a road map that leads you directly to your goal. Ensure this road map is detailed and specific as we've discussed so far, so you can avoid any uncertainties along the way.

At the beginning of your game plan, you had a goal of losing ten pounds by graduation, which is June 1st. You know your obstacles (parties, cravings, peer pressure, etc.) and you have identified the people you are going to work with and the knowledge you need to gather. Now, you must outline what you need to actually do from now until graduation to reach that goal. For example, maybe you decide that you are going to have to discipline yourself to eat three small meals a day, cut out any junk food, exercise daily, drink 100 ounces of water a day, keep a positive mental attitude along the way, etc. All these actions need to be written down and reviewed periodically so you can make sure you are making progress. They are each mini goals within your major goal of losing ten pounds by June 1. And now you have your game plan developed—congrats!

9) Describe how you will feel once you have reached your goal.

This is typically an enjoyable step for most. You are nearing the end of the steps and by now you have put a tremendous amount of thought and energy into your goal. Now take a minute or two to think about how you will feel once you have reached it. Writing that feeling down by hand (paper and pen, not computer or phone app) will help you to tangibly imprint this feeling on your brain. Keep this feeling in your mind at all times—think about it as you go to bed, when you wake up, and as you navigate your days. It will keep you going when the going gets tough and on track toward your goal even when you don't feel like it, or on the days when it just gets hard.

After you lose the ten pounds, you should feel a whole lot better about yourself. More confident. You will look much healthier to yourself and others and be bubbling with vitality. Your attitude toward yourself and others will improve. To most, these attributes would be of sufficient value to pursue your goal. But the only one who can answer that is you.

10) Start Now!

Now that you have finished steps one through nine, you are ready to go. Get that game plan in action. Not tonight or tomorrow, but right now. Get to it and do it!

Each one of these steps, excluding step ten, needs to be written down and reviewed as often as possible to remind you about your goal and why you are pursuing it. If you don't write them down, you may as well not even attempt them. I know that sounds a bit harsh, but it's true. Committing something to writing is when it starts to be imprinted on your brain at a much deeper level. Writing it down is when things start getting real.

When I wrote the first edition of this book in 1991, I had a sign on the wall in front of my writing station that said, "Goal To Reach Before Graduation—Finish Book." I had a similar sign in the bathroom, so not a day went by that I was not reminded several times of my goal to finish writing this book by the time school ended in May.

If you methodically think through and write down steps one through nine, you can be assured that you will reach your goal. You can also be assured that if you don't write them down, your goals and dreams will remain unattainable. Look, of course the writing alone is not going to get you to your goals; you still have to take action to get there. But writing it down is absolutely crucial to the doing.

There's a story that in 1953, Yale University began a goal-setting study of that year's graduating class. They found that 87 percent of that year's graduating class did not have any concrete goals upon graduation. Ten percent had goals, but they either weren't written down or weren't specific enough to act on. Only three percent of the graduating class actually performed all the necessary steps required to reach a goal.

Twenty years later, Yale did a follow-up study to see what became of the 1953 graduates. They found that the only graduates ones to reach their goals (of those who even had goals to begin with) were the ones who performed all the required steps. They also found that this three percent were more financially secure and made it further in their careers (two easily measured performance levels) than the rest of the graduates put together! So, if you have goals you want to reach during your lifetime, I strongly suggest that you perform the ten steps described above.

While doing research for the rewrite of this book, I was not able to find any verified documentation of the above Yale study. In fact, it now appears to have reached the status of urban myth. I decided to include it here anyway because real or not, it had a profound impact on my own personal experiences over the last almost thirty years.

When I was first exposed to story of the study thirty years ago, it was one of the reasons for me initially writing down my own goals while in high school, again in college, and subsequently at other points in my life using the ten steps in this chapter. These activities, of focusing on planning my goals and then writing them out, have led to my achieving many, many goals I don't think I would have achieved without them. I have made connections, and had insights and amazing life experiences that I would not have had otherwise. And my observation of the results experienced by other people, young and old, who have executed the above steps is that of wild goal attainment and abundance. So while that particular Yale study is more myth than reality, the very real results I personally have experienced and observed in others is as real as it gets.

The first time you try these ten steps, make your goal something easy to attain in a short period of time—say thirty days. That will give you practice so when you do make a commitment to a long-term goal, you will be sure-footed and know exactly what to do.

You must have goals!

I really like these ten steps. It sure sounds like they work. Anything else I need to know to augment the ten goal steps?

You bet.

DON'T CONFUSE ACTIVITY WITH ACCOMPLISHMENT

Here's what I mean. Just because you are busy all day doesn't mean that you are any closer to your goal. I have a friend who is so busy that she has two phones attached to her hip at all times so her family and friends can get in touch with her separately from her business contacts. She is one of those people who is invariably late for her appointments because she "got tied up." The problem is that at the end of the day, she still hasn't really accomplished much. She is what many would call a "Jill of all trades and master of none." Each day, she makes the same mistake of scattering her energies instead of focusing on accomplishing something substantial. You may remember that this is what I was trying to warn you against at the end of the diversity chapter. If she learned to concentrate on one thing at a time, she would get done in half a day what it now takes her an entire day to do.

To demonstrate the power of concentration, try this little exercise:

Use the stopwatch on your phone to time yourself and count out loud from 1 to 26 as fast as you can. Write down your time. Now time yourself saying your ABCs, also out loud, from A to Z, as fast as you can. Write down your ABC time. Add your number-counting time to your ABC time and write that down. Next, time yourself saying out loud, as fast as you can, your ABCs combined with counting from 1 to 26, interchanging the letters and numbers like this: "A, 1, B, 2, C, 3, D, 4..." and so on until you finish with "Z, 26." Write that time down.

Compare your combined time of saying your ABCs and numbers separately with the time of saying them interspersed. What do you see?

Yup.

Focusing on one thing at a time is *way* more efficient than any type of multitasking, no matter who you are. So while you think you are able to intersperse reading texts or social media posts with studying for an exam or writing a paper, the science is clear that yes, you indeed are doing both activities, but you are doing neither activity as well or as efficiently as you would if you separated the tasks out and performed them one at a time.

Please never forget that little lesson; it will be true for the rest of your life, in every aspect of your life.

Choose a time every evening to look back on your day to make sure you have accomplished something. It would also be a good idea to take a look at your written goal game plan (step seven) at the same time to make sure you are on target toward the successful completion of your goal. This is a simple exercise that can be done right before you fall asleep and will help to keep you pointed toward the attainment of your goal. It's like a little review for yourself. The act of doing this every night allows your subconscious to work on your goal while you sleep. Set up a recurring reminder on your phone or watch if that makes it easier for you. If you let it slip, you may also find yourself slipping away from the path of reaching your goal.

You must have goals!

CONCENTRATE YOUR ENERGIES

While you are working toward your goals, there will be many times you will need to concentrate your energies to an intense degree. When I say intense, I mean it. During those times, you will need to put everything else out of your mind except your goals. That isn't easy to do, but it is extremely effective.

As I have already mentioned, my goal before I graduated college was to finish writing this book. In completing this task, there were many times when I would rather have been doing something other than sitting in front of my computer typing out pages. There were times, especially toward the completion of the initial draft, when I wrote during the early morning hours when I would much rather have been in my warm bed, snoozing away. But I forced myself to wake up early to write on those days because I knew, for instance, that the rest of the week would not afford me much chance to write.

If I had decided *not* to get up those mornings when my alarm went off at 6:00 a.m. (which I came very close to doing many a time!), I would have been behind schedule in the completion of the book. Yeah, I would have been able to sleep a couple hours more, but I would be cheating myself out of reaching my goal. What kept me going during those times was the thought of actually having a published book I had written while I was still in college. That thought was so cool to me that it helped me do things like get up at 6:00 a.m. and work on it instead of just rolling over and dreaming until 8:00. Step nine in action right there.

If you learn to take time during the day to concentrate all your energies, powers, and thoughts on the attainment of your goal, you will find that you also have time to do other things that are important too. As I mentioned earlier, this is not an easy skill to master, but if you attempt and even come close, you will lead a more fulfilled life. For example, because I got up those mornings and worked on the book, I had time in the evenings to relax and hang out with friends. If I had not gotten up early, I wouldn't have had a good time those evenings because I would have felt like I was slacking off on my writing.

Many of today's thought leaders say that when a person is in the pursuit of a goal, she should free her mind and body of all thoughts and actions that don't pertain to the attainment of that goal, at least until it has been reached. Ralph Waldo Emerson once wrote, "Distractions always un-tune us for the main purpose of our lives." This thinking is probably a surefire way to get you to your goal, but it's also a surefire way to become more narrow-minded than you may want to be.

I believe that if you live, sleep, and eat your goal for an extended period of time, you run the risk of tiring of it and maybe eventually abandoning it altogether, or even worse—abandoning the important people around you. Giving up on your goals for those reasons is unhealthy and will counteract your many other efforts at achieving success and well-being.

I also believe that we should concentrate our energies not twenty-four hours a day, but rather when needed, as I did to hammer out those words for you. We should let our goals be our passions and let our hobbies and other activities enhance our lives but not detract from our goals. That way, we can both achieve our goals *and* have the diversity and experiences in life that are important to us.

I'm glad you said that because I was starting to think you wanted us to do anything to reach our goals, even if it meant giving up other important things in our life. I do want to make and reach goals, Jason, but I don't want to stop the rest of my life to do so.

I understand, and that is precisely why I stress concentrating your energies only when needed and in short bursts.

Every once in a while, hobbies and activities will temporarily sideline your goals, but you must possess enough discipline to make sure that it is *only* temporary. Don't allow yourself to become distracted from your dreams or you will find yourself at age forty-five or so, wishing you had stuck to your goals instead of making your temporary sidelines permanent.

People have said that John D. Rockefeller's genius was that he could concentrate all his energies, powers, and thoughts on one thing for five minutes. Rockefeller was involved with so many different activities, he didn't have time to deliberate over things for a great deal of time. He needed to concentrate all his energies on different subjects, one at a time, take care of them properly, and move on. Because he was able to concentrate effectively in short spurts like that, he was free to partake in other interests.

Some motivational teachers like to compare the concentration of our energies to a fire hose. They say that when all the water is forced out of the nozzle (we concentrate our energies), we get great power, but if the water is divided into a spray (we diversify our energies), it falls softly to the ground with no force. In other words, if we concentrate our energies, we are capable of achieving great things, but if we scatter our energies, we don't create much effect toward what we can accomplish at all. But the comparison must be extended to make a complete and meaningful picture.

Here's that full picture. You don't need a fire hose until there is a fire. Therefore, you should only need to force (concentrate) your energies out of the nozzle until the burning need to accomplish something to reach your goal successfully is put out. Then you can concentrate on another goal, or you can put the hose away and relax for a while to take part in other activities. I believe that is why Rockefeller needed to concentrate on one idea for only five minutes at a time. If you learn to concentrate correctly, those five minutes will be sufficient to put out the fire.

Don't underestimate the importance of concentration; without it, you likely will not get what you want in life. If you learn to concentrate your efforts, nothing can stop you from making your dreams and goals become reality. I just don't believe that you need to concentrate twenty-four hours a day, because if you do, you will ruin your all-important diversity. An example is the entrepreneur who spends so much time and energy on his business that he neglects his family and ends up getting divorced. Yes, his concentration level is high and his business may be doing well, but he sacrificed his family for it.

No goal or business in the world is worth losing your loved ones.

How would you suggest that I choose my goals? I know that the answer will be different for everyone, but is there any general information that may help me?

There sure is.

THE OUTSIDE OF THE ENVELOPE

AT THE BEGINNING of the movie *The Right Stuff*, a group of pilots in the 1940s were vying with one another to be the first to fly a plane faster than the speed of sound—about 767 miles per hour. Until then, it was thought to be impossible to break the sound barrier. In the movie, each pilot would try to take his plane "just a little faster" every time he went up. They had to be careful, though, because the planes at that time were just barely equipped to handle the speeds they were going, and no one really knew what would happen if they did actually break the sound barrier. Each of the pilots referred to his attempts at going just a little faster as "pushing the outside of the envelope," always trying to do a little better than the time before.

What method should you use to choose your goals? Some experts say to make high, lofty goals and shoot for the moon. Some even have funny names for this technique, such as making BHAGs, or "Big Hairy Audacious Goals." The rationale behind this is that if you don't quite make it to the moon, you'll probably land on a star, which ain't so bad. I like the rationale, but the idea of knowing up front that you probably won't hit your goal doesn't sit right with me. I've seen a lot of disappointment in people who don't hit their too-lofty goals, and that can lead to guilt, shame, and self-confidence issues.

Others suggest making your goals down-to-earth and realistic. That way you won't have to go through the disappointment of not reaching your goals; they should be relatively easy to reach. The challenge here is that you end up not pushing yourself to the betterment you're seeking. How do I know this? You've read this far in this book, so I know you're seeking something better for yourself and you're willing to put in the work to get yourself there. Realistic goals will do a good job of keeping you average, but you want more than to be average.

The method I use when I create my personal goals, and when I coach my clients, lies somewhere between the above two methods. Maybe we can call it the Goldilocks Method. I try to push the outside of the envelope in creating my goals. With each new goal, I give myself the challenge of imagining how I can push myself to do just a little better and greater each time. My goals aren't so lofty as to be unattainable, but they are far enough outside my comfort zone to force me to take on new and exciting challenges. Then, when I reach my goal, my comfort zone is widened and I become a more well-rounded, more equipped, and more diverse person. Then, with my next goal, I push the outside of the envelope a little farther. I am always moving ahead and broadening my horizons.

This is so exciting. I have some great goals in mind and I want to go out and tell everyone about them.

Before you do that, here are a few more suggestions.

WHOM TO TELL

This is a very important subject, so heads-up.

You should be very choosy with whom you share your goals; it can make or break your success. Here is an easy rule of thumb to follow while you're deciding whom to tell.

First, you must realize that there are two basic types of goals. One is the type in which you are trying to give up something, such as smoking or cussing or eating junk food. The other is the type in which you are trying to do things to improve yourself, move up in the world, or separate yourself from others in some way. This could be a goal such as running in a marathon, obtaining a better job, or becoming a millionaire.

The first type of goal, in which you are trying to give up something, should be told to as many people as possible. I mean *everyone*, even people you don't particularly like. The reason to do this is because once you tell everyone that you are going to stop eating junk food, you are pretty much locked into doing it. If you don't, you would be looked upon as somewhat of a loser with no self-discipline. Just kidding—kind of.

On the other hand, you need to be selective about to whom you tell your move-up-in-the-world goals. That's because most of these goals are nurtured by support from others and can be destroyed by too many other elements. Take the underprivileged young man whose dream is to be a doctor. One day he tells his friends that he plans to study as hard as possible so he will be able to reach his dream. But his friends don't have his vision; they subsequently make fun of him and tell him that he will never be a doctor because he is not smart enough, or his family isn't wealthy enough for medical school tuition, etc. The next day his friends give him more reasons why he can't become a doctor, such as, "nobody like you grows up to be a doctor and it ain't cool to study anyway." Daily negative influences might bring that young man to give up his dream altogether. If he just went along quietly and studied his butt off and did what he needed to do to get into a good college with a good pre-med program, he may have been a doctor one day. But because he told the wrong people about his dream, the dream died. His friends didn't have similar great aspirations, so they made sure that they ruined his. Maybe they thought they were helping him by constantly giving him a dose of "reality"; maybe they didn't want him to succeed where they didn't see a path for themselves. Either way, their negative voices were too loud for him to withstand.

There are always going to be people around who will want to give you 101 reasons why you *can't* do something. I guess people just don't like to see others around them succeed or do great things when they aren't succeeding themselves. You must watch out for jealous people as you pursue your move-up-in-the-world goal because they will try to kill it just as quickly as you try to attain it. That's why you should reveal these goals only to people you are sure will support you. If there is any doubt in your mind about their support, don't tell them. The person you want to tell is someone who unselfishly cares about you and loves you and will be excited for your success.

When I first began writing this book I only told two people about it: my parents. I was positive that they would be 100 percent behind me in my effort and give me encouragement when I needed it. I also knew they would keep my goal confidential, which was important to protect me from those outside negative voices I described.

Telling your move-up goals only to supportive people is crucial, especially when you first develop your goal. That's when you're most vulnerable to negativism. When you can see that success is imminent, whom you tell becomes less important. By that time, you will be so strong in your conviction to reach your goal that nothing should be able to stop you from doing it. During the writing of the first draft of this book, when I had about 150 pages written and I knew I would be finished with it in less than a month, I happily told more and more people about it. I knew that even if I did get negative reactions to my work at that point, it wouldn't knock me off course.

FINAL THOUGHTS

I HOPE BY now you understand why I said at the beginning of this chapter and throughout that you absolutely, 100 percent, must have goals! Without them, you just sort of drift along, which won't do you any good if you want to live an exciting and fulfilling life. I want to finish with some final thoughts on goal setting and goal getting.

1. **When you do reach your goals, immediately set new ones.** That will keep you pushing the outside of the envelope and improving.

2. **Be sure to always have several goals "on the go."** Keep yourself moving forward and diversified.

3. **Make a significant commitment to your goals.** As I mentioned before, sometimes you will have to suck it up and concentrate, and that's OK. You'll pay the price in hard work now, but you will enjoy the benefits when they come later—and oh, will they come!

4. **Make your goals measurable.** Measuring helps you gauge your progress while you're working. Step seven is a good place to do that.

5. **Remember, you can't play the game of life without any goals, and you can't hit a target if you don't have one.**

6. **START NOW!**

BONUS! BONUS! BONUS!

It's funny. Even with the ten steps outlined above, we sometimes still need a super easy point of entry when it comes to goal setting and goal achievement. We've thought a lot about that at our coaching company, Rewire, and we've developed a free solution called *The 30-Day Sprint*. The Sprint is a goal setting/goal getting program in a tidy thirty-day package in which you receive an email a day for thirty days, giving you an easy-to-accomplish, ten-minute task. On day one, you start to get your mind right around where you currently are versus where you want to be. Day two includes another easy ten-minute task, and so on. By day thirty, you will have accomplished your goal. It's crazy how easy and effective it is!

Wanna join The Sprint? Visit www.rewireinc.com/30-day-sprint-.

START NOW!

What will YOU do as a result of reading this chapter?
YOUR Thoughts on Goals

CHAPTER EIGHT

LUCK

Luck is what happens when preparation meets opportunity.

My friends used to come up to me sometimes and say, "Jason, you're so lucky. Everything you do always seems to come out the way you want it. How did you get that way?" I tell them that my luck started with my being born into a great, big family (twelve people total; really—twelve). Then I tell them about my first encounter with luck.

When I was twelve, I asked my parents for an Atari 2600 for my thirteenth birthday. The Atari 2600 was the first widely available video game system that could be played on a home television. Man, I wanted that thing so bad I could taste it. Not to mention that "every cool kid in the neighborhood had one." Unfortunately, my parents' answer to my plea for the Atari was a resounding NO! I was upset, but I didn't argue because in my family it was understood that when my parents said no (which wasn't that often), they meant no. My thirteenth birthday came and went. I got the hand-held Mattel Football Classic video game. While this was a pretty badass game at the time (look it up), it wasn't the prestigious Atari 2600.

Fast forward a month and what do I see on the back of my Cap'n Crunch Cereal box? An advertisement for a contest they were holding. Guess what the first prize was? Yup—an Atari 2600. Without hesitation, I begged my parents for permission to enter the contest. After all, I only had to send in three Cap'n Crunch Cereal box tops. No problem for a kid who ate a box a week. "Sure," my parents said. "In fact, you can enter as many times as your little heart desires." My parents were just humoring me by letting me enter the contest. They figured the chances of my winning the Atari were so low, they had nothing to worry about. Boy, were they wrong! Two months later, a thin envelope arrived in the mail addressed to me from Cap'n Crunch himself. I had won the Atari! I was absolutely ecstatic. I could not sleep for days. For some odd reason, my parents did not exactly share my excitement. They still weren't too keen on my having the game, but how could they go back on their word at this point? Two weeks later, the UPS man delivered a big brown box to my doorstep with the coveted Atari 2600 inside.

OK Jason, nice little story, but where is the point?

The point is this: If you desire something or set a goal for yourself, whether it be an Atari 2600, a new car, or financial independence by the time you graduate from college, don't stop striving until you have exhausted every single option to obtain it. At that point, hit the Reset button and start all over again. Don't stop until you have actually attained that specific goal. Don't let your setbacks or mistakes get you down or stop you dead in your tracks. Instead, use setbacks as a learning tool for what *not* to do the next time around. Good luck comes to those who capitalize on opportunity.

I'm here to tell you right here and now, this idea that I'm putting in front of you is *way* easier said than done, and you need to know that. As you're striving toward your goals and true desires in life, there will be storms, bumps, bruises, naysayers, signs that doors are closing in all directions, setbacks, etc. When these things happen, I'm asking you to lean in even harder, get even more creative, and find other directions. And know that at the point at which it is the most difficult and you're leaning in as hard as you possibly can—right there at that point, you are in the company of greatness and just about to see a crack of light that is the "luck" you're seeking.

My father raised me with the old saying, "If at first you don't succeed, try, try, and try again." A great example of this comes from the invention of the light bulb. After 1031 unsuccessful attempts at burning a filament with the use of electricity to no avail, someone asked Thomas Edison why he still pressed on with his idea. He corrected the question by replying that he had not been unsuccessful with his 1031 attempts, but rather had successfully found 1031 ways *not* to burn the filament. He knew that there is no such thing as a chain of problems that never comes to an end. A very common idea in business circles is that "failure is never fun, but sometimes you have to fail before you succeed."

Please don't confuse setbacks as a sign that "it wasn't meant to be." I'm observing more and more these days, especially with the younger generations, that the setback is the point at which people start telling themselves that they didn't really want the thing they were working toward in the first place. Sure, there are times when this may be the case, but more often than not, this is simply an easy way for them to let themselves off the hook. DON'T LET YOURSELF OFF THE HOOK! You're better than that. You know how I know? The fact that you somehow got engaged with this book and have read this far into it tells me that you've got what it takes to persevere. You're strong enough for that. I know you are and I believe in you.

Am I getting the point across to you? Temporary failure is inevitable. It's a must. Just like you must breathe to live. There is no problem with temporary failure. The problem occurs when the temporary failure keeps you from your goals because you allow a temporary failure to become a permanent one. And the only person to blame for this permanency is yourself. UFC champion Conor McGregor said, after his first championship loss, "It's not really much of a big deal—you brush it off and come back. Defeat is the secret ingredient to success." You either win or you learn.

This type of thinking needs to become ingrained in you, needs to become part of your everyday lifestyle, but don't for a minute think it will be easy to attain. It's hard to "fail" repeatedly. But know that it is certainly attainable. It's like anything else: The more you do it, the easier it gets. You know, practice makes perfect.

When you reach a level of success, however you decide to define that, you will begin to notice that people start to talk about how much luck you have, and how things just seem to come out the way you want them to. And, yes, you will actually be lucky, but only because you made that luck yourself. Your self-made "luck" is borne and nurtured through your persistence. I can't emphasize enough how important persistence is. As Calvin Coolidge said:

> *"Nothing in the world can take the place of persistence. Talent will not; nothing is more common than unsuccessful men with talent. Genius will not; unrewarded genius is almost a proverb. Education will not; the world is full of educated derelicts. Persistence and determination alone are omnipotent."*

START NOW!

What will YOU do as a result of reading this chapter?
YOUR Thoughts on Luck

CHAPTER NINE

ORGANIZATION

My observation is that organization is one of the most important keys to the development of a successful person. You have heard of the absentminded, disorganized professors, such as Doc in the movie *Back To The Future*, or you see a parent's and/or teacher's cluttered desk. You may even think that they are pretty successful even though they seem to be a little sloppy with their paperwork. My dad, for example, was an established physician (now retired) and private real estate investor in our area, but if you took one look at his desk in his office, you would think he couldn't be established at anything but moving papers from one spot to another (not to mention what hit the floor in the meantime). He says that he could put his hands on anything he needs at his desk right away, and usually he can. Every once in a while, though, I would ask him for something that was probably on his desk, and it took him a while to find it for me. Not a big deal, maybe, but what I am about to relate to you is.

This doesn't happen often, and if I said that it did, I would a) be lying, and b) have one retired physician and private real estate investor on my tail. You see, every once in a long while, my father would misplace a bill on his desk—say the credit card or water bill—which, of course, needed to be paid by a certain date. Well, that date rolled past without the bill getting paid, not because of my parents' inability or unwillingness to pay, but rather because they just didn't know about it. It was lost somewhere in the shuffle on my father's desk. So next month's bill came with a late charge on it. My parents didn't understand at first why it happened, but with a little research, they found the problem and paid the bill—late charge and all. Still no big deal, right? Well, kind of. Let's say the late fee was $25 and this situation happened three times a year. There's $75 out the door for no real reason at all. I would rather put that $75 where it will help earn interest for me, or even go out to dinner with it. Is $75 a large amount of money? Maybe not. But let's say you made this mistake each year of your life and you live another seventy years. That's $5250 wasted in a lifetime! $5250! That is indeed a lot of dough.

I do understand that since the initial writing of this book in 1991, there are all kinds of auto bill-pay apps and online payment conveniences that can help curtail the above scenario. I also know that whether we are talking about a desk cluttered with paper or a cluttered online bill payment system that is not properly organized, the end result can be the same. And those are the kind of negative results I'm attempting to steer you away from.

But where does this fit in my life?

Organization does not include just the neatness of your desk or work area. It is important to be organized in almost *every* aspect of your life. Keep in mind, though, organization is not regimentation. Being flexible in the event of unexpected occurrences throughout the normal course of a day is key. I have been accused of being too regimented at times, but I have learned over time that flexibility can sometimes be more important and essential to my future than what I had initially planned anyway. Flexibility in the work arena is a must. And being a flexible person opens you up to some of the spontaneous serendipities of life, and that can be just plain old fun.

Here are some suggestions that will help you become a more organized person:

1) Take some time each evening to make a list of the tasks you want or need to achieve the next day.

This usually will only take five minutes or so. Write down the people you need to call, the errands you have to run, when you will be working out, what time you have to be at work or school, and other tasks you'd like to get done. That five minutes will give you a chance to think about the next day and provide it with some structure. I favor writing these things out with paper and pen; research has shown (and I've already mentioned), when you write something down on paper, it tends to stick in your brain better. But I'm also flexible enough to understand that apps such as Get It Done, Todoist, and Evernote can work really well for people too (see what I did there—"flexible"—get it?).

For example, here is one of the lists I made for myself as I was writing this book:

call Dr. Franklin
call Loyola about computer
go to bank
get info about hunting safety class
get car fixed
work on book
take check to Meredith
write thank-you notes

Some say that putting your list in order of priority is also a good idea. I disagree because I think that could make you feel as if the things at the bottom of the list aren't very important, causing you to put them off until another day. This is how the seeds of procrastination are planted. I only put on my list what I know I can handle in a day. If something needs to be done later in the week or month, I make sure it hits my calendar on a specific date in the future. The main point here is to get this stuff written down, because if you don't, you will inevitably forget it. I once heard that a short pencil works better than a long memory and have since come to find that this is very true. Even if you are sure you will remember to complete a task, write it down anyway. It doesn't take much time at all and you surely won't forget something important if you have a note reminding you of it.

A list like this can be compiled on a weekly basis as well. For instance, Sunday afternoons or evenings are a great time to take a look at the week ahead, and to double-check the things you have coming up. It allows you to make adjustments ahead of time. This proactive preview of the week helps you focus on what will be going on, and set proper expectations for yourself. Is there a test coming up that you should be studying for? Exactly what time are you working on Wednesday? And oh yeah, there's a party on Friday. You get it. This activity list has been a lifesaver for me and for those who are close to me because it helps me prepare myself for what the upcoming week looks like.

2) Keep good records and keep them in one central spot.

Good record keeping is 100 percent essential to keep up with your financial life, but it is also important for other aspects of your life as well. Years ago, I started to keep a file on just about everything I do. Yes, I'm talking about real, hard copy files here, not the files that live on your computer or in the cloud. And no, I am not a fanatic about files. It just makes things easier for me. What kind of stuff should you be putting in a file? Some examples of what I keep in files are:

- receipts, warranties, and service agreements for any purchases that may, for some reason, have to be returned or repaired
- automobile information and records
- boat information and records
- insurance records
- children's school information and records
- any information that has to do with taxes (i.e., giving statements, pay stubs, receipts, etc.)
- passports, social security card, birth certificate
- any other type of legal documents
- all the research I gathered for the writing of this book

This list is definitely not all-inclusive. Any time I need any important papers, I know exactly where I can find them. Instead of spending precious time looking for them under my bed, in my desk, or some other random place, I just open my file box and there they are. Go to Amazon or Walmart and get yourself an inexpensive file box, along with some file folders, and try it out. I'm sure you'll be happy with the results.

I get it. Some of the items above can be kept in electronic files instead of hard copy ones, and that's cool too. But you'll want to be as organized with the soft copy files as you are with the hard copy ones for the time-saving element mentioned above. Also, know that as great as technology is, there are still some things for which only a hard copy will do. There will most certainly be a time in the future when just about everything is digitized, with the use of blockchain, etc., but as of the time of the writing of this book's second edition, a hard copy passport is the only way to enter and exit foreign countries.

Again, keeping records is not hard to do and creates great lifelong habits that you will come to appreciate. Plus, you'll be a happy camper with your excellent record keeping when your computer, bike, watch, lamp, or whatever breaks and you still have the warranty and receipt to get it fixed without additional charge.

3) Be neat in general.

The best place to start is in your bedroom. I know I will catch static for this because many of your bedrooms are, as was mine sometimes, a plain mess. Try it, though. Pick your clothes up off the floor and put them in your closet. Make your bed each morning (which can be your first win of the day, setting up a "win after win" day), and maybe even dust once in a while. Yes—dust. When most people try for neatness, they find that they actually feel better about themselves and more in control of themselves and their surroundings. It may be hard at first if you have to go through an initial cleaning. But after that, it's as easy as cake as long as you don't let it build up again. And you can make the initial cleaning a little easier by using the K.I.S.S. method. Remember that?

Some of the young adults I interviewed on this topic thought that "the ease and peace of mind this [being organized] creates goes well beyond the minimal time it takes to put into effect," and "I always feel like I have my life together after cleaning my room or organizing."

Your parents will be happy when they walk into your room, either at home or school, and find that it's neat. It's also true that clean and neat living quarters are key when trying to impress someone you're interested in. That's more than twenty years of experience talking, but try it out and let me know the outcome.

After cleaning your room, move on to your car, if you own one, or just yourself in general. If you carry yourself in a neat and crisp manner, it won't be long before people will begin to sit up and take notice.

4) Be on time for everything.

I dedicate this suggestion to my mother. If she has taught me anything in my life, it is the absolute importance of being on time. She even takes it one step further and says to be there, wherever there is, at least ten or fifteen minutes ahead of time. I can say with certainty that I was never late for anything when Mom was driving me around before I got my driver's license. Thanks, Mom.

I want you to be there when you are supposed to be there. If you say you'll meet someone at 5:00 p.m., make sure you're there at 5:00 p.m., not 5:03. I'm really serious about this. If you don't show up on time, people will start to think of you as an unreliable person, and that's a bad rap to have. I don't want anybody wondering about whether I can or can't be counted on just because I don't show up on time. If you run into a situation where it is impossible for you to make an event on time, definitely call/text/whatever to let someone know you're running late. That doesn't make up for your lateness, but it does show the other person that you care and value their time.

I'm sure you have heard that the first impressions people get of you tend to stick, and they will govern how people always think about you. The initial element to a great first impression is to be on time. Think about it. If you show up to a job interview even five minutes late, you've probably already lost your chance of getting the job, before you even open your mouth. Whereas, someone who showed up on time, but maybe gave a so-so interview, might get the job instead. That would be terrible.

When I was in high school, if anyone showed up to lacrosse practice late, he knew to start running laps around the field. That was the punishment for being late, and it was up to the coaches when he would stop running (running, mind you, not jogging). A teammate once had to start running at 4:03

(practice started at 4:00), and he wasn't called to join the rest of the team until we did our end-of-practice calisthenics at 5:45. You can be sure that not many guys came to practice late after that incident. Be on time for *everything*!

I hope these suggestions help you. Not all of them will fit your particular needs completely, so pick and choose. Use them to your advantage in every way possible, and fold them into your own existing organization techniques.

Remember, also, not to be *so* organized and regimented that you lose focus and miss out on other important things in life, such as having fun. I believe God put us here on earth for many things, and one of them is to have fun. So please have at it, and don't let your over-organization or over-anything-else become obsessive. You have to learn to strike a balance with your priorities in life. I'm not sure that any book can teach you how to strike that balance; each person is so different from the next. It's something you're just going to have to organize yourself.

START NOW!

What will YOU do as a result of reading this chapter?
YOUR Thoughts on Organization

CHAPTER TEN

DISCIPLINE

"A dead thing goes with the stream, but only a living thing can go against it."

—G. K. CHESTERTON

THERE AREN'T MANY things in this book that can help you unless you also possess one very key characteristic.

Discipline.

I have come into contact with many different successful people, and they all have different personalities and character traits. It is difficult to pin down any one thing, if there is only one thing, that makes one person more successful over the next. Are you born with whatever "it" is, or do you grasp "it" through some type of learning experience? Most indications point to a little bit of both, but...

While I have not been able to figure out exactly what it is that makes one person successful and the next not, I have observed that successful people do share in common an enormous amount of discipline. This discipline drives them when the going gets tough, as the going always does. It keeps them on track even when the temptation to swerve a little is there and it pushes them ahead while others are telling them that they should slow down or maybe even stop.

The neat thing about discipline is that it is nothing more than a state of control over your own mind.

On the surface, this concept may sound pretty simplistic. I mean, who doesn't think that he has control over his own mind? But in reality, discipline is one of the most difficult traits to master.

Why is it so difficult?

It's difficult because every single one of us has a plethora of outside forces that are forever pulling us in many different directions, such as Netflix, YouTube, email, texts, Snaps, games, the music we listen to, the friends we hang around, the environment in which we live, the books and magazines we read, the cars we drive, our parents or guardians, our teachers, our coaches, and that all-consuming smartphone that is constantly begging for every minute of our attention. In fact, the phone in your pocket, while amazing and life-changing in several different ways, is also literally *built* to grab your attention. Seriously. Our phones, apps, and games are *designed* with solid neuroscience in mind to make them as addictive as possible!

Some of these forces mentioned above are positive and some are negative. In fact, the very same forces can be positive in some situations and negative in others. That is exactly where the difficulty begins.

You must learn to immunize yourself against the negative forces and only permit your mind to let in the positive ones. That takes a major amount of discipline. I mean, a *major* amount. Without discipline, you will be subject to the whims of whichever forces you come in contact with on a daily basis, good or bad. And if this happens, you will become the equivalent of a dead fish being pulled by the current, whichever way it takes you. Do you want to be a dead fish?

No.

Neither do I. Every spring and summer, salmon swim upstream to where they were born so they may spawn. I have seen these salmon runs in person and they are absolutely amazing to watch. The fish swim against strong currents and even up little waterfalls to get where they want to go. Their determination is pretty remarkable. It would be so much easier for the fish to succumb to the negative forces of the strong currents they go up against. Instead, they struggle their way against the force of the water because they are driven by something much more powerful. Their triumph comes when they reach the spot where they were born so they can spawn, as their species has done for millions of years. Now, let me ask you again, do you want to be a dead fish that goes wherever outside forces pull it, or would you rather be like the salmon, with enough drive to go against outside forces to get where they have to go?

I would rather be like the salmon, of course, but the salmon swims upstream because it was born with the instinct to do so. I don't think I have an instinct that gives me that type of discipline. So how do I acquire the discipline to make me successful?

We aren't as fortunate as the salmon in this regard. We don't automatically possess discipline the way they do by instinct. But the point is that if you train yourself in self-discipline, it can work for you the same way as instinct does for the salmon. It can drive you to overcome any obstacle put in your way.

But we must go out and acquire our discipline. Oh, and sorry to let the cat out of the bag here, but it's usually not so easy to just "go out and acquire it." Self-discipline is formed over time and with practice. But you do have the ability to start small and start now. Here's what I mean: Let's say you wanted to complete a three-mile race, but you've never even run across the street before. It is highly unlikely you will decide to run that race one day and then go out and actually run and complete it the next. But you could go out and buy a pair of running shoes today. And then create the small discipline of putting on and lacing up those running shoes for, say, one week straight. No running in them yet. Just get comfortable with putting on the new shoes and walking around the house in them for that first week. Once you start to feel comfortable there, you could then stack on the discipline of walking around the block in those same running shoes for a week, then walking around two blocks the next week. By week four, maybe you're walking around one of the two blocks and jogging the second one. And so on and so on, until you are running a full mile (which is just awesome, by the way!). You then build, similarly slowly, to two miles, and then to three until you are able to run the full three miles, repeatedly and comfortably. By now you'll have the discipline (maybe it's even a habit by this time) of getting outside and running, and before you know it, you'll be running in that race you signed up for.

The example above is not a particularly quick or easy one, and there are bound to be challenges along the way, but you will have acquired a discipline for yourself, gotten a few wins to celebrate along the way, and run your race to boot!

As in the above example, discipline is a learned habit that needs to be constantly worked on to keep it functioning. Remember, discipline is control over your own mind. This mind control comes from realizing that your first duty in life is to yourself. Think of the admonition made on airplanes to secure your own oxygen mask first, before you help others. That is a hard concept for many, including myself at times, because we can get too caught up in the daily craziness to have time to grasp the idea.

But you need to safeguard yourself against the negative forces that life throws our way, which includes protecting your mind, body, and soul. For example, are you limiting the amount of social media (or alcohol, or food, etc.) you are consuming daily? Are you getting enough sleep? Are you hanging around the right people (remember chapter two)? Are you regularly moving your body and eating enough vegetables? Not having this protection can lead to the dead fish syndrome. This protection becomes much easier when you understand that your first duty in life is to yourself.

I am not saying I want you to be selfish, to disregard everyone else. You just need to be true to and protect yourself first, because only then will you be equipped to be true to everyone else. Think about it. If you weren't concerned about yourself, how could you ever be truly concerned about anyone else? So, having self-discipline has nothing to do with slighting anyone else or only thinking about yourself in a self-centered, selfish way. In fact, it's just the opposite. When you take excellent care of all facets of yourself first, you are then able to present your best self to those around you and the greater world, *and* you are in the best shape to serve and take excellent care of those around you.

I know that if I was having brain surgery, I would want the surgeon who is taking care of herself and getting excellent rest each night to perform my surgery over the doc who regularly has a few drinks in the evening and doesn't get enough sleep. See what I mean here?

Because discipline is learned over time, the only way to make it part of your day-to-day life is to practice it again and again and again. And you need to practice it and practice it and practice it until it becomes a habit. The best way to practice is to think of something you want to do and then just stick to it until it's done. Use something easy at first.

For example, let's say you want to start making your bed in the morning. The reason you don't now is because you never seem to have enough time in the morning, or you forget, or whatever else. Start telling yourself that you are going to make your bed each and every morning, no matter what. Then do just that. Sounds quite easy and it really can be, but the test will come when you wake up fifteen minutes late one morning and are rushing around to get to work or class on time. If you don't make your bed on this particular morning, that means you still need to work on obtaining more discipline. If you do make your bed on that hectic morning, you are well on your way to being a finely tuned person of discipline on the path to success.

Jason, if I'm rushing around in the morning to get to class on time, I am not going to worry about making my bed just because I told myself I would. Getting to class on time that particular morning will be more important to me than getting my bed made.

Getting to class on time *should* be more important to you than making your bed, but recognize that you are sacrificing your self-discipline because you couldn't get your butt out of bed two minutes earlier.

Once you've practiced and gained some discipline at an easy level, move your practice to a higher level. It's up to you what you choose, but one way to really practice discipline (that many people attempt and fail at every year) is to adopt a regular exercise program. If you can get yourself on a regular exercise program and stick to it, you will be killing two birds with one stone. Your discipline will get to the habit stage and you will benefit by being a fit person who feels great and is positioned to present your best self to the world, able to serve that world with abundance!

Discipline is the stick-to-itiveness to control your own mind. This is what will lead to the actions and results you're looking for. Once you have enough of that stick-to-itiveness to fend off the negative forces trying to push you off your road to success, you will be in excellent shape. But please be sure to take advantage of it now while you are young, rather than waiting until you are older and have already been through a life of shuddas and wuddas. The decision is yours.

START NOW!

What will YOU do as a result of reading this chapter?
YOUR Thoughts on Discipline

SECTION THREE:

HOW WE ENGAGE MONEY

CHAPTER ELEVEN

MONEY

Most financial planners and many financial publications agree that ages twenty-five through thirty-four mark the time when you should master basic financial skills, acquiring good habits of spending, saving, borrowing, giving, and investing.

My observation is that your financial education is a lifelong journey that needs to start as early as possible—as in right now if yours has not officially begun yet! Whatever your age, *now* is when you need to start mastering basic financial skills. The earlier you learn about money and basic financial skills, the better chance you have of acquiring good habits instead of trying to break bad ones later on.

In school, you will (if you haven't already) learn cool things about money such as how it originated from the barter system, how the Federal Reserve System works, and maybe even what the discount rate is. This information is important to know, and I'm glad I know it, but that knowledge doesn't immediately and directly affect my personal bank account. I'm interested in teaching you as much as possible about your personal money, the money that flows in and out of your hands, so that you may eventually have more and more of it. This should sound a little more appealing to you than learning about the discount rate. I know that personal money management was far more appealing to me when I was younger, and it is the reason my present financial life is not the disaster that many people face these days.

FACTS

While doing research for this book, I came across two interesting statistics regarding personal finances (https://www.gobankingrates.com/retirement/planning/why-americans-will-retire-broke/), and they both tell me that we need to change something and quickly: as of 2018, 42 percent of Americans are on track to retire broke, and 57 percent of millennials have $10,000 or less saved for retirement. WHAT!?

Can you imagine working hard your whole life and, toward the end of it, having absolutely nothing to show for all that hard work but empty pockets? These are not acceptable facts for me, and I hope they aren't for you either. This is exactly why it is so important to start acquiring this information now, while you're young.

WHAT'S THE DEAL WITH MONEY? FIRST OF ALL...

Money plays an incredibly important part in your life, whether you want to admit it, think about it, or acknowledge it or not. Without money, you can't clothe yourself or eat or provide shelter for yourself. Maybe more to the point for you, you can't go to the movies or a concert or out on the town if you don't have any money. Money gives you the freedom to do these things. Yes, freedom. In fact, if you don't have any money at all, you probably won't be able to survive in our society. In other words, you would most likely die without money! So money is actually very important, and it looks as if it will remain that way for a long time. So you must get with the program and at least get the basics down now, because if you don't, you are essentially waiving your right to freedom. Sure, there are ways to live incredibly cheap and even some "off the grid" techniques to get away from many of the needs for money, but for the bulk of you reading this book, money will be playing a very important part of your life. This chapter, along with the remainder of this book, assumes that importance.

WHAT ELSE?

Be careful not to get so overzealous about money that you turn people off. Money is very important, but it represents different things to different people. It doesn't take much money to make some people happy. I heard it said best when I overheard two older men talking about the significance of money. After one said that money doesn't give you an automatic ride to happiness, the other responded with, "Yeah, but it sure does grease the wheels."

A large sum of money ("large" meaning different things to different people) isn't always necessary for someone to be happy, but money does give the ability to make life both more secure and more enjoyable. Money is a conduit to getting what you want from life, a way to get from here to there. For example, if you want a boat, or a house, or to go on a trip across town or around the world, you will need money.

If you have respect for money, or if you just want some ideas on how to make the best use of and get the most from your money, the following chapters will be helpful to you. I'll begin with the basics: finding your net worth, keeping an expense diary, budgeting, and why you should start your financial planning now. Intertwined with the basics are some simple yet integral subjects about money that many people, especially young adults, don't know much about. The main reason most young people, or anyone for that matter, don't know very much about money is because we are not taught about it on a regular basis. Many people, such as my father and subsequently me, know about money and finances only because we have devoted time, energy, and yes, money to becoming educated on these subjects. The keys to a successful financial life are therefore "secrets." They must be secrets, considering 42 percent of Americans will retire flat broke!

During the writing of the first edition of this book, I came across statistics from the Consumer Federation of America that stated that the average score on a basic financial literacy survey of 2010 full-time college juniors and seniors was only 51 percent. A person should be able to score at least 25 percent just by guessing!

During the current rewrite some twenty-five-plus years later, I was eager to see what the data says now about young adults and their financial literacy. By many measures, it's become even worse! Here is some example data from a paper I found (https://scholarcommons.usf.edu/cgi/viewcontent.cgi?article=1138&context=numeracy) written by Carlo de Bassa Scheresberg while he was serving as the Senior Research Associate at the Global Center for Financial Literacy:

—Only 34 percent (WAY less than half!) of young adult survey respondents were able to correctly answer three simple questions designed to assess financial literacy.

—In 2009, college seniors graduated with an average credit card debt of more than $4,100.

—Students who borrowed for college and earned bachelor's degrees in 2011 graduated with an average of $26,600 in student loan debt.

—65 percent of surveyed respondents misunderstood or were surprised by aspects of their student loans or the student loan process.

It's hard for me to remain calm when I read the last two sentences in the summery of Scheresberg's paper:

"To summarize, there is a growing gulf between the amount of financial responsibility given to young individuals and their demonstrated ability to manage financial decisions and take advantage of financial opportunities. Hence, financial illiteracy remains a significant obstacle to both financial market efficiency and to full participation of young people in the current financial environment."

Were the students who took these surveys just stupid?

Of course not. They just hadn't yet been exposed to many things financial in their lives. It is part of my mission to change that—right here and right now, as you are reading this book. It is my philosophy that the educational system of our society can do, and does for the most part, a very good job of producing a well-rounded person. But when it comes to producing people who will be financially comfortable when they retire, it stinks! You'll need to learn these financial secrets on your own until I, and others like me, raise enough havoc to get things changed in our school systems.

It is my intention to share these secrets with you now, so you won't need to experience hard times just to learn what works and what doesn't, or to live a lifestyle that is restricted by your financial situation. The earlier you learn these secrets, the earlier you'll be free of the financial barriers that hold so many people back.

DEFINITIONS

Here are some terms that will be helpful for you to know while reading the next few chapters:

Gross Income/Earnings—Your total income before taxes or any other deductions are taken out.

Net Income/Earnings—What you end up with after subtracting all your income taxes and Social Security taxes from the total of your wages, investment earnings, and any other income you may have.

Budget—A written projection of how you want to allocate your future income over a specific time period.

Tax—A compulsory payment for the support of the government. Tax is usually a percentage of income, property value, sales price, etc.

Asset—Something you own that can be sold for cash or traded for another item of value. Think your car, computer, bike, jewelry, savings, and stocks, and any other investment.

Liability—A debt. Liabilities can include credit card balances, car payments, girl/boyfriend (just kidding), student loans, and any other personal loans.

Net Worth—The difference between your assets and liabilities. If your assets exceed your liabilities, your net worth is positive and it feels excellent! If your liabilities exceed your assets, your net worth is negative and it stinks.

Liquidity—The ability to sell your assets and receive cash quickly.

Cash Flow—The stream of money passing through your hands. When you spend more than you earn, which none of you will be doing from this point forward, you have negative cash flow (booooo!). When you earn more than you spend, you have positive cash flow (yay!).

Interest—The amount you pay for the privilege of borrowing money.

Collateral—Anything used as security for a loan—such as a car or a house.

Market Value—The amount that someone is willing to pay you for an asset. If the highest price someone will pay you for a car you are selling is $6,000, then that is its market value.

This is by no means an all-inclusive list of the financial terms you should be familiar with, but it does give you a start and a reference as you read the next four chapters.

START NOW!

What will YOU do as a result of reading this chapter?
YOUR Thoughts on Money

CHAPTER TWELVE

NET WORTH

WHAT KIND OF financial situation are you in right now? Do you owe people money? Do people owe you money? Do you even know? How are you keeping track of this type of information? Overall, are you in the hole or are you keeping your financial head above water? The answers to these types of questions must be established before you can begin to modify or start new financial habits. You need to take a snapshot of your present financial life—even if it's a simple picture. The best way to get this snapshot is to determine your net worth. It tells you right away if you're in good or bad shape and to what degree. Determining your net worth is easy. The following exercise can be done on apps or websites such as https://www.nerdwallet.com/blog/finance/net-worth-calculator/.

My suggestion for the first time you calculate your net worth is to grab a pen and paper and follow the simple steps below. It will most likely take you less than fifteen minutes, and by doing it initially by hand, your brain will be able to better concentrate on the meaning behind the calculations as opposed to just getting to the end result without fully understanding the bigger picture. So grab a pen and paper and let's get started.

1. **Make a list of everything you own.** I mean *everything*, including your checking and savings accounts, cars, furnishings, appliances, artwork, clothing, jewelry, devices, laptops, sports equipment, instruments, any investments

you may have, and anything else you can think of that you own. These are your assets. Easy so far, right? Well, it stays that way.

2. **Next to the name of each asset, write down its present market value (see the definition of market value in the previous chapter).**

3. **Add up the market value of all your assets and write the total at the bottom of the page.**

4. **On a separate page, list the names of all your creditors.** These include anyone to whom you owe money: this could include your car payment, your parents, rent, student loans, credit cards, etc.

5. **Next to the creditor's name, write the amount owed to each.** These are your liabilities.

6. **Total up your liabilities at the bottom of that page.**

7. **Subtract your total liabilities from your total assets to arrive at your net worth.**

So, how did you do? Hopefully, you're on the positive side. If you are, congratulations! You're on the right road and things will soon be getting even better. If you're not, it's OK (especially because you're young), but you're going to have to do some work to get on the positive side. Although certain debt is good, which I'll explain later, you never, *ever* want your net worth to be negative. That is just asking for trouble. If you have a negative net worth, it means you are spending beyond your means, and continuing to do so will eventually lead to a financial downfall. It can sneak up on you like a snake and bite you unexpectedly.

George S. Clason is the author of what many believe to be one of the greatest financial books ever written, which explains in parables the key secrets to financial success, *The Richest Man in Babylon* (first published in 1926, it is still in print today). In it, Clason describes a camel trader named Dabasir, who spent beyond his means in his younger days. The setting is 8000 years ago in the great city of Babylon. This is what Dabasir has to say about himself in his youth:

"Being young and without experience I did not know that he who spends more than he earns is sowing the winds of needless self-indulgence from which he is sure to reap the whirlwinds of trouble and humiliation. So I indulged my whims for fine raiment and bought luxuries for my good wife and our home, beyond our means.

"I paid as I could and for a while all went well. But in time I discovered I could not use my earnings both to live upon and to pay my debts. Creditors began to pursue me to pay for my extravagant purchases and my life became miserable. I borrowed from my friends, but could not repay them either. Things went from bad to worse."

I hope you learn from Dabasir that spending more than you earn will indeed make things go from bad to worse. As I've said, it will sneak up and bite you when you least expect it. Fortunately, things worked out OK for Dabasir, but only because he heeded some of the financial secrets you are in the midst of learning. Things will work out for you as well if you practice the important financial skills explained over the next few pages.

If you have a positive net worth, my guess is it is probably below $10,000. That is quite OK, though, because many young adults have a negative net worth. So you're already ahead of the game. The first time I figured out my net worth, when I was nineteen, it came out to be $6321. And more than half of that was my half ownership in *Stealth*! Without *Stealth*, my net worth would have been a mere $3,071. Not so impressive, but on the positive side, nonetheless.

Whether your net worth is positive or negative, you now need to make sure you are moving in the right direction (toward positive). One way to do that is to refigure your net worth every six months and keep a record of it every time, so you can keep track of your progress. That way, if you do digress, it will be easy to find out exactly where you went wrong and make the necessary corrections along your journey.

HOW DID I GET THERE?

We now know where you stand financially. The next thing to do is figure out how you got there. The most thorough way to do that is to keep a detailed income/expense journal for a month. In this journal, you'll want to write down everything you do with money. I mean *everything*. The day you get paid or receive your allowance, write it down. When you buy an ice cream cone, write it down. When you go out to a bar and spend $21.65, write it down. When you buy stamps, write it down. Get the picture? Every time you receive or spend money that month—you guessed it—write it down. By the next time you get paid, you should be able to account for every penny from the last time you were paid.

Each entry in the journal should include the date, a description of the expense or income, and the amount of the expense or income. Some example entries might be:

8/11/19 — Gave Logan money for lunch (Expense) — $10.00

8/14/19 — Received credit card reward from VISA (Income) — $120.63

8/16/19 — Paid AT&T MasterCard for July (Expense) — $551.17

8/16/19 — Bought lunch at Quiznos (Expense) — $10.19

8/17/19 — Paid toll for Chesapeake Bay Bridge on the way to the beach (Expense) — $2.50

Just like the net worth exercise, you can keep this journal in the notes section of your phone or use an app such as mint.com, but for the initial thirty days, I suggest you journal these entries by hand in a notebook or on a piece of paper. This manual entering of your income and expenses will force you to pay the most attention to your finances. But if this manual entry suggestion seems like too much for you, do it the way that suits you best. I'd rather you do the exercise your way than not do it at all my way.

After you've kept your journal for thirty days, you'll be able to clearly see where your money is coming from and where it is going. It will allow you to pinpoint places where your money is leaking away; leaks such as impulse shopping and lunches out will be revealed, and discovering them will allow you to take action to plug them. For example, I could have eaten lunch at home on 8/16 for about a third of what I paid to eat at Quiznos. When these leaks are revealed and plugged, you won't find yourself saying things like, "Last week I made three hundred dollars and now I only have one hundred, but nothing to show for the other two hundred."

The idea behind keeping this diary is to educate yourself on exactly how you're spending your money. I want you to be very aware of the money that flows in and out of your hands, and to learn to control your spending, if that's what's needed. This control is almost impossible if you don't know what you're doing with your money in the first place, but rather easy once you do.

OK, so now I'm educated about how and where my money comes from and where it goes. What do I do now?

If you have a negative net worth, you should be able to see why it is that way by referring to your income/expense journal. You should also be formulating ideas about how to curb some of your spending (the leaks) to change that negative number into a positive one. If your net worth is positive, you should be very excited to find even more ways to help build your net worth to new heights.

So, what's next?

Read on, my good friend.

START NOW!

What will YOU do as a result of reading this chapter?
YOUR Thoughts on Net Worth

CHAPTER THIRTEEN

THE MILLION-DOLLAR PLAN

So what do I do with all the money I'm saving by curbing my spending? You still haven't told me how I'm going to live the lifestyle I want while not having to worry about money along the way. How do I get rich, Jason?

Let's make a plan. A budget, if you will. I'm not going to give you exact numbers and figures, except for one, because every person's situation is different and what works for one person may not work for the next. What I will do, though, is give you guidelines that will put you on the right track and help you along the way when you need it. Read this chapter over and over again until you're sure you fully understand it. It will help make you very wealthy if you let it.

10 PERCENT RULE

THE VERY FIRST step that should be taken, once you know where you stand financially, is to follow the 10 Percent Rule, which is so easy to follow, it's surprising. Don't let the simplicity fool you, though; it is, without a doubt, the most important and powerful financial secret I can give you. The truth is always simple—remember the K.I.S.S. method?

To follow the 10 Percent Rule, all you have to do is *always* save a minimum of 10 percent of your gross earnings. So for every $100 you make, you would save $10. And for every $1000, you would save $100. It's a piece of cake! It really is. If you put this money away immediately (the same day you receive your earnings), you won't even miss it. In fact, it's easy to have your employer deposit that 10 percent into a separate investment or savings account for you. If your employer doesn't offer that service, or if you're self-employed, you can set up an automatic transfer from your regular bank account to a separate savings or investment account. It's important that you make this step automatic; if you don't even see that money, you won't be tempted to spend it. If it's an automatic process, this is a step you don't need to think about. It's just happening for you in the background, helping to create wealth while you live your life.

After over thirty years of practicing the 10 Percent Rule, I have yet to come across a time when I have missed the 10 percent I put away. It's like paying an income tax to yourself. The cool part is that you, and only you, reap the benefits from this "tax." That makes it a little different from the income tax you pay to the government.

There are two important stipulations for this rule to work properly. One is that you can never skip saving the 10 percent. Not during the holidays, not when you're buying a car, not when you're going on spring break to Daytona and you think you may need some extra spending money, not when you need "just a little more cash" to buy that "really cool" bike, not ever. Each and every time you earn money, put away 10 percent of it immediately!

The second stipulation is that you don't spend any of that savings.

So what the heck do I do with it?

You invest it, which I will discuss later. That second stipulation is very difficult for most people to follow. It's so tempting, when you see your savings climb into the hundreds and even thousands of dollars, to go out and treat yourself to a new toy like a wave runner, or the latest and greatest iPhone. Don't yield to those temptations. Your future self will be so happy you didn't yield that you'll call me to thank me a hundred times over.

You might be a little confused at this point, but just bear with me and read on.

I'm really only a little confused, but you know, I think I've read or heard about this 10 percent thing somewhere before. Did you make up this rule or did you get it from somewhere else?

I didn't originate this rule, but have adopted it and practiced it faithfully. In fact, this rule has been around for hundreds, maybe even thousands of years. Just about every financial planner I know preaches the 10 Percent Rule. But there are only a select few, including some of those same financial planners, who actually *follow* it. It's one of those common sense "secrets" that I spoke of in the intro of this book. This rule seems to be so easy to execute that hardly anyone does it and, therefore, hardly anyone is independently wealthy! Please, be one of the "hardly anyones" and heed the rule, along with the rest of this chapter.

EMERGENCY FUND

OK Jason, I just made $200 and 10 percent of $200 is $20 and here it is. How do I... I mean, you won't let me spend it, so what do I do with it?

I'm glad you asked. Deposit that twenty dollars into your

investment account, which I will show you how to set up in chapter fourteen. Keep putting 10 percent into this account until you have $2000 put away. The first $1000 of this account should be earmarked as your emergency fund. The purpose of this money is just what it sounds like—for emergency purposes *only*. Justin Timberlake (or Guns N' Roses, for you classic rock fans) coming to town doesn't constitute an emergency situation. Your car breaking down or you losing your job does. Understand?

Many financial advisers suggest saving at least two months' living expenses in your emergency fund, some say six months, others even suggest a year's worth. If this emergency fund idea is new for you, start with $1000 and adjust that number as your journey in life (and income and needs) change over time. I count my blessings often that I have not needed to use my emergency fund to date, but it sure is nice to know it's there if needed. It's worth having just for the feeling of security it gives.

INVESTMENT TIME

THE OTHER $1000 should be used to make your first investment. I'm not going to give you specific advice on where to invest your money because that is so unique to each person. But I will give you some broad, yet key, suggestions about investing:

1. **If you have a job where your employer offers a 401K or an IRA, that should be the place you start investing because many employers will match deposits (can you say free money?).**

2. **If you don't have a job that offers a 401K or an IRA, open an IRA yourself, because the earnings in an IRA are not taxed until you withdraw the funds during retirement.**

3. **Always be sure you have the proper security for your investment.** And by security, I mean some sort of collateral against your investment such as the stock or real estate itself. Safety is key when investing money, especially at the start of your investing journey.

4. **Don't be seduced by the promise of rapid wealth from "opportunistic" investments or "turn-key" business opportunities.**

5. **If it sounds too good to be true, it probably is.**

6. **Read all documentation pertaining to your investment carefully and make sure you fully understand everything about the investment, even the tiny, hard-to-read, fine print.**

7. **Don't forget that you are young, and some people in this world unfortunately love to take advantage of inexperienced investors.**

The list of reading material at the end of this section provides an exceptionally good source to refer to when looking for ideas on how and where to invest your money.

The only people giving you advice on investments should be those who have proved to be knowledgeable and successful about investing and those who are licensed to do so. The proof of this knowledge should be obvious by their success in their own personal investment portfolio. Never, ever take advice about money from someone who doesn't have any. Even if it's your grandfather and you highly respect him, if he doesn't have any money himself, then don't take financial advice from him. If his advice hasn't worked for him throughout his many years, there is no reason to believe it will work for you. I know this sounds harsh (especially when talking about your grandfather), but you must get the message or you may take bad advice from a person who is broke and risk ending up broke yourself. Again, the reading material at the end of this section is a good place to start, but always make sure to check out each investment yourself.

I got the message, Jason. What's next?

Let's assume you have made your first investment and you are receiving interest or income from it. All income from your investment needs to go directly back into the investment account, along with your ongoing 10 percent, until the account grows enough to make a second investment, and then a third, and so on. This will be an automatic process if you invested in a 401K or an IRA, but may need to be manual if you have another form of investment, like real estate or something else. Although your account may start slowly—let's face it, 10 percent of your earnings now is likely to be much lower than it will be later on—it will soon grow by leaps and bounds, literally. Stick with the 10 Percent Rule religiously, and when you find yourself with a little extra cash (holiday gifts or monetary graduation gifts, etc.), dump some, or all, of it into your investment account. If you make this tiny commitment to yourself now, your money will increase over time and eventually start to multiply. Many, many, *many* self-made wealthy individuals in the world began their fortune by first saving (with a system like our 10 Percent program) until they had enough money to begin investing.

PUT YOUR MONEY TO WORK MAKING YOU MORE MONEY

Now I'm on my way to riches. That sounds great and all, but exactly what is going on here? How does this happen and what do you mean, "it will soon grow by leaps and bounds"?

To put it simply, what is happening is that this money invested, *your* money, is working for you instead of you working for your money. Most of us have been brought up to believe that if we work hard, we can earn enough money to buy a house and, together with a spouse or partner, support each other and our 2.5 kids along with Fido. You know, the live the "American Dream." So we work to get the money that allows us to live that dream. We are taught to work for our money.

The problem arises when we want a little more than that dream normally provides, or we want something a bit different. For example, what if you wanted to take a year off from work to travel around the world? The answer is that you probably wouldn't be able to take off for a year because if you did, you wouldn't make enough money to pay your bills, let alone pay for the trip itself. OK, maybe you don't want to travel around the world, but wouldn't it feel great to know that you could do something like that?

If you follow the 10 Percent Rule, you end up having your money work for you instead of the opposite. Each time you make an investment, you are putting your money to work to make you *more* money. And if you start now, this phenomenon gets really cool over time. Personally, I like the idea of my money working for me to put food on the table over time.

But right now my parents put food on the table. Why should I worry about putting food on the table when I am so young?

Just wait until you are on your own. I don't want you to *worry* about putting food on the table now. But I do want you thinking about it a little now so you will be fortunate enough never to have to actually worry about it later.

THE MAGIC OF COMPOUNDING

FOLLOWING THE 10 Percent Rule coupled with good, sound investing and discipline allows your money to work harder for you than you could ever work for your money. You see, the money you invest makes more money, and then this new money reinvested makes you even more money. You will find that your money will start multiplying like rabbits. This multiplying that you will come to love is called the magic of compounding.

It's crazy how this works! Check it out:

If you invest the principal sum of $100 in an investment that earns 10 percent per year, at the end of one year you will have $110. This $110 is called the future value of a hundred dollars invested at 10 percent for one year. At the end of the second year, you will have earned 10 percent, but this time on the $110 you have after year one. This comes out to $12 earned in the second year. So, the future value of a $100 invested for two years at 10 percent is $122. And the future value of $100 invested at 10 percent for three years is $135. After the first year, your money grows faster than the ten dollars you earned in the first year, and each succeeding year it keeps growing at a faster and faster rate. You are earning interest on your principal amount ($100) plus the additional earned interest. This accelerated growth, my youthful reader, is the mechanics of the magic of compounding.

Remember the $1000 I'm having you invest? Let's take a look at a chart that shows the future value of that $1000 each year for forty-five years if we found an investment that yields 16 percent. I'm using forty-five years because most of you are probably around twenty years old right now, and forty-five years from now, you will be around sixty-five. If you are younger than twenty, you're in even better shape, because you have even more time to compound your money. If you are older than twenty, don't sweat it, because at least you're smart enough to start the compounding now. Sixteen percent, by the way, is a very realistic yield today for some investments, such as real estate.

I think you are wrong about that, Jason. My parents don't receive anywhere near 16 percent on their mutual fund or on any of their other investments. And when I look online, I don't see a lot of investments yielding 16 percent.

Not so fast. Sixteen percent was, and still is, a very possible yield, and I'm not talking about earning this yield in risky junk bonds either. I'm talking about good, sound investments, mostly in real estate and mortgages. I know this sounds aggressive but stay with me for a minute. Let's take a look at the chart:

Future Value Of $1000 Compounded at 16%

Year 1—$1,172.27	Year 10—$4,900.94
Year 2—$1,374.22	Year 11—$5,745.23
Year 3—$1,610.96	Year 12—$6,734.96
Year 4—$1,888,48	Year 13—$7,895.20
Year 5—$2,213.81	Year 14—$9,255.32
Year 6—$2,595.18	Year 15—$10,849.73
Year 7—$3,042.25	Year 16—$12,718.82
Year 8—$3,566.35	Year 17—$14,909.91
Year 9—$4,180.72	Year 18—$17,478.45

Year 19—$20,489.48
Year 20—$24,019.22
Year 21—$28,157.03
Year 22—$33,007.66
Year 23—$38,693.92
Year 24—$45,359.75
Year 25—$53,173.91
Year 26—$62,334.23
Year 27—$73,072.59
Year 28—$85,660.87
Year 29—$100,417.70
Year 30—$117,716.70
Year 31—$137,995.90
Year 32—$161,768.60
Year 33—$189,636.60
Year 34—$222,305.40
Year 35—$260,602.20
Year 36—$305,496.30
Year 37—$358,124.40
Year 38—$419,818.80
Year 39—$492,141.40
Year 40—$576,923.00
Year 41—$676,310.00
Year 42—$792,818.40
Year 43—$929,397.90
Year 44—$1,089,506.00
Year 45—$1,277,196.00!

OK, OK, now you got my attention. You mean to tell me that if I invest $1000 now at 16 percent, in forty-five years it will have compounded to over a million dollars?

Yes. There are no tricks here, you don't have to be lucky and win the lottery or be overly intelligent or have rich parents or anything like that at all. You only need enough self-discipline to religiously follow the 10 Percent Rule, which includes methodically investing your savings and reinvesting your after-tax earnings from those investments. If you don't reinvest your earnings right away, you will lose some of the magic of compounding. Because you have a million dollars at stake here, I'm sure none of you want to interrupt the cycle and lose that magic.

The astounding thing about this chart is that it takes into account only your first $1000 investment. Because you will be continuously saving 10 percent of your earnings, you will have even *more* money to invest after that. The possibilities of how much money you could have in the future are miraculous if you can train yourself to use enough financial discipline now, while you're young. And it is so very easy. You only need to make $10,000 a year to save $1000 (10 percent of $10,000) every single year. Many of you reading this right now make that much per year with just a part-time job!

Let's say you're still not comfortable using my 16 percent-investment-yield example. Yields change over time, but at the time of the rewrite for this book, the average yield for mutual funds was 7 percent. If you continually invested $300 per month, and those investments yielded and compounded at 7 percent, you would hit the million-dollar mark in about the same amount of time, forty-three years. Three hundred dollars may sound like a lot of money right now, but it gives you a couple of different options for accomplishing the plan. The idea is to keep moving in the right direction. You'll certainly get a lot closer to reaching it than if you do nothing!

One last thought as we wrap up this section. If you are still in doubt about how important this compound effect is on your life, here is what one of the best minds of the modern era, Albert Einstein, had to say about compound interest:

> *"Compound interest is the eighth wonder of the world. He who understands it, earns it ... he who doesn't ... pays it."*

Yep.

IS IT TOO GOOD TO BE TRUE?

THAT DEPENDS ON you.

I think we've established that compounding interest is truly magic. How you begin the compounding is not magic at all—rather basic, in fact—but not necessarily easy to actually implement. The 10 Percent Rule, along with the rest of your plan, will set you up for much greater financial success than just about anything I know. But there's no free ride to get you there. The only way you'll get there on a free ride is if you are lucky enough to get a huge inheritance (which you should never, ever count on anyway) or win the lottery, or some other similar event. I'm sorry to drop the bomb on you dreamers out there, especially because I'm a dreamer myself. But you have to take the initiative with, and have the discipline for the 10 Percent Rule, and you must work to earn your initial money.

I thought you told me that I should have my money working for me instead of me working for my money.

Yeah sure, but you have to get the ball rolling for yourself with this plan and work for the money to begin your investing. If you are afraid of work, there is almost nothing in this book that will be of any help to you. Yes, just like everyone else, you are going to have to work to earn that dough. But the difference is that you now have a plan that most people don't. Instead of spending your money throughout your life and not having any left of it later, you are going to have more than a million bucks to do whatever you want to do. Sure, you are paying your dues along the way, but isn't it worth it? The dues aren't even that steep! Once you get in the habit of putting away that 10 percent, you won't miss it a bit. In fact, everyone I know who follows this plan has never complained of ever *needing* their 10 percent.

PAYING YOUR DUES

Like it or not, every single one of us has to pay our financial dues sometime in our lifetime. Either you pay yours now, while you are young and full of vitality, or you will pay them when you're old and gray—you get to choose.

Not all, but most everyone will have a period in their life when money is a bit tight. If you can get through that period early in life by passing up things like driving the fast cars and taking the exotic vacations and the other expensive fun things, you will have the opportunity to have money later in life. Money being tight is gentler on the young than it is on the old.

The above statements are smart thinking, but I for one like to have my cake and eat it too. And my desire for you is to be wealthy when you're older, but I also would like you to enjoy what life has to offer along the way. The only catch is figuring out a way to be able to do both. I'm pretty sure I've got it figured out.

Wait a minute. Before you tell me how you got it figured out, let me point out that sometimes we are unable to choose when we pay our dues. Unexpected occurrences arise that are out of our control: emergencies, car repairs, home improvements, sickness, etc.

Such a great point. The emergency fund we've spoken about should take care of most of your unexpected expenses, but larger expenses sometimes do occur and must be handled promptly and properly. I don't have a fix-all answer to all life's quirks that might send you off-track financially (no one does), but I can give you some tools so you can get through these upheavals as smoothly as possible. This next tool, for example, allows you to pay most of your dues smoothly, keeping their weight as light as possible.

PACE—THE KEY TO LIGHTENING THE LOAD

THE 10 PERCENT Rule is the best answer I have found that allows us to seriously lighten the burden of the financial dues we all have to pay at some time or another. Ten percent regularly taken out of your earnings won't change your lifestyle. It just won't. For example, if you earn $300 a week, you are only taking out $30 to invest. You can live essentially the same lifestyle whether you make $300 a week or $270. So yes, you still pay your dues, but the burden most people face is not yours because you are starting so young and pacing yourself for the rest of your life. And therein lies the key to this whole idea—pace!

In the mile run, the winner is not the person who bursts out right from the start and uses up all her energy only to fizzle out at the end. The winner is the runner who paces herself and is consistent throughout the entire race.

The same thing is true in the financial race. The winner is not the person who lives an extravagant lifestyle from minute to minute, only to find himself penniless later in life. Nor is the winner the person who slaves to save an exorbitant amount only to become frustrated and upset because he deprived himself of a comfortable lifestyle. The winner is the one who, like us, saves not a lot, but a little, and then paces these savings over a long period of time. And the fact that you are starting so young makes the situation that much more manageable!

I cannot stress enough how easy it is to save this 10 percent. As I said before, 10 percent taken out of your earnings shouldn't affect your lifestyle a bit. And because this is true, you are successfully making the burden of your financial dues as light as possible.

It's starting to come together now, but the only thing I still don't understand is this: When do I actually get to spend and enjoy this money that I'm going to save over the years?

DON'T EAT YOUR SEED CORN

THE BEST ANSWER I've got to this valid question goes something like this:

Let's say you really like corn—I mean you really love it—and you want to grow it so you will be able to eat corn whenever your heart desires. Someone is generous enough to give you one kernel (seed) of corn to plant so you can grow your own. You plant it in the spring and tend to it, and in the summer your cornstalk grows and produces two ears of corn, just as expected.

Now you have a decision to make. If you eat both ears of corn, you won't have any seed corn to plant next year, and your corn-eating days are over. But you can satisfy your desire for corn by eating just *one* ear (which is more than you had before someone gave you the original seed corn) and plant the seeds from the other ear next spring. If you do this, you will be in great shape because every ear of corn has at least 100 kernels on it. You decide to eat one ear now and plant the other.

Next spring arrives and you plant your 100 seeds, and in the summer, your 100 seeds produce 200 ears of corn. To make the story more realistic, let's say the crows ruin 95 ears of your corn. So you are left with 105 good ears. Decision time again. This year, you decide to enjoy yourself a little more than last and you eat five ears and save the other 100 for planting next spring. So now you have 10,000 seeds of corn for planting (100 ears x the 100 seeds on each ear).

The third spring, you plant your 10,000 seeds. Because you always learn from your mistakes, this year you put up a scarecrow so the crows won't ruin so much of your crop. In the summer, you have a potential harvest of 20,000 ears of corn, minus what the crows may eat. You are now at the point where you can eat all the corn you could ever want for the rest of your life and still have more than enough to plant each year. And it has taken only three years to get to this point!

And here's a kicker: Each ear of corn really has closer to 800 kernels, so the real math on this is even crazier. The moral of the story is, don't eat your seed corn. If, in the first year, you had eaten both ears of corn, you would be out of luck from then on as far as corn-eating goes. What a tragedy for a corn lover such as yourself!

Nice story. When do I get to spend my money?

OK, OK, to find the exact answer, let's look more closely at the similarities between this example and our 10 Percent Rule. The first seed of corn equals your first $1000 investment. Just like the first two ears of corn the first seed provided, if you spend your profits from your first investment, you stop the growth cycle, ending the compounding before it even gets a chance to start.

Instead, you reinvest your profits, just as you did your seed corn, to keep the growth going. Each year you do that, you really aren't suffering financially because you are still able to spend the other 90 percent of your income. Again, just like the corn, this 90 percent should grow each year because your regular income will likely grow through raises, advancements, etc. The cycle continues, allowing the magic of compounding to take place. Therefore, don't eat your seed corn!

The answer to when you get to spend your money is the same as when you get to eat your corn. You decide when you have enough money to do what you want. In other words, there is no "one size fits all" answer for everyone. The answer depends on you as an individual. Look at the chart on pages 133 and 134 to find out how long it will take you to produce the funds you feel comfortable with. Be careful not to cheat yourself. Don't let others talk you into spending your savings before you've reached your goal amount. If someone had talked you into eating that other ear of corn the first year, you would potentially never have been able to eat corn again. The exact same thing happens with money. Once someone talks you into spending any of your savings (and many will try), your chances of ever being a millionaire, or reaching financial freedom as defined by you, are slim.

IS THIS REALITY?

Jason, the plan sounds great and I want to get started ASAP. Just tell me one more time if this plan is reality or not. I don't want to get psyched up about something that won't really happen. I'm in school and I don't make much money at all. If I follow your plan, will I really become financially independent?

I stake my reputation that if you follow the 10 Percent Rule exactly as I have outlined, you will be a very wealthy person one day. Will you struggle at times, especially in the beginning? Yes. But remember that anything worthwhile is going to take some work. You will probably even mess up a little in the beginning. That's OK. We all mess up a little when we try something new. So if you make a mistake, just forgive yourself, get back on the saving and investing horse, and move on.

KEEP. MOVING. FORWARD. WITH. THE. PLAN.

This 10 Percent Rule can work for anyone. It doesn't matter if you're young or old, black or white, shy or outgoing, male or female, educated or not. The rule is blind to all these things, as we all should be. The rule won't work to the same degree for everyone, simply because nothing does, but it will work for every single one of us to some extent. You just need to stick with it, through good times and bad. Be dedicated and persistent and the rule will work for you.

PERSONAL 30-YEAR CASE STUDY

I have followed the 10 Percent Rule since before the initial writing of this book and I can confidently tell you that it works!

It worked for me and it *will* work for you. I told you in the introduction of this book that my net worth was greater than two million dollars. As I wrote, and re-wrote, this book, I struggled with the decision to put those numbers in print for you, because my parents taught me to be humble and anonymous in financial situations. But in this particular case, my thought is that if you, the reader, can clearly see the words I wrote more than twenty-five years ago and compare them to today's results, maybe, just maybe, that will inspire you to take similar actions yourself to obtain similar results.

Over the last thirty years, there have been market ups and downs. I have experienced many amazing highs in my life and my family, including the birth of our amazing children, Julia, JJ, and Sadie. But I have also endured some of the lowest of lows, such as Sadie's death. But through all the highs and all the lows, I've continued to stick to the 10 Percent Rule and now, as an adult, I am living proof that yes, indeed, the plan works!

Now, my question to you is, what will you do with that information?

This chapter included some heavy lifting, so let's summarize.

SUMMARY

Following the million-dollar plan means that you are:

- Continuously putting away 10 percent of your after-tax earnings every single time you earn money, forever and always.
- Using the first $1000 or so of your savings for an emergency fund, and drawing on this fund *only* if an emergency arises.
- Using the next $1000 of your savings to make an investment earning a yield (a rate of interest) you are happy with. Make sure to get investment advice only from successful investors who can prove that they know what they are talking about.
- Putting any after-tax money earned from your investments right back into savings, along with the continuous flow of 10 percent, until your savings grows enough to make another sound investment. You will now begin to experience the magic of compounding with your money working for you!
- Not eating your seed corn.
- Enjoying life to the fullest.
- STARTING NOW!

Recommended Investment-Related Readings:

- *Richest Man In Babylon,* by George S. Clason
- *I Will Teach You To Be Rich,* by Ramit Sethi
- Anything by Dave Ramsey or Ric Edelman
- *Your Money Or Your Life,* by Vicki Robin
- *Building Wealth One House At A Time,* by John Schaub
- *How To Personally Profit From The Laws Of Success,* by Sterling W. Sill
- *You Can Get Anything You Want,* by Roger Dawson
- *Wall Street Journal*

START NOW!

What will YOU do as a result of reading this chapter?
YOUR Thoughts on the Million-Dollar Plan

CHAPTER FOURTEEN

HOW AND WHERE TO BANK

MANY OF YOU already have some type of savings account and maybe even a checking account. Whether you do or don't, it's OK; this chapter will help you decide where your money should be deposited, or at least spur some ideas for you on this subject. I will suggest a way for you to set up and structure your accounts, and then give you some brief information on the different institutions available for these accounts. This particular banking program has worked wonderfully for me for the last thirty years, and I have observed others with a similar banking program also profiting from it over the years. The magic in the system is that it's simple, and it only consists of two initial accounts: a savings account and a fun account.

THE SAVINGS ACCOUNT

THIS IS THE account where you deposit your savings, which is the money you will eventually invest to start that whole magic-of-compounding thing. Lots of magic going on around here!

Remember the 10 Percent Rule? Well, this is where your 10 percent goes. Before any money is spent from my non-investment earnings, I first put 10 percent of those earnings into my savings account. Non-investment earnings include your pay or your allowance, etc. Always, and no matter what, at least 10 percent of your non-investment earnings should go into the savings account. *All* of your investment earnings, after-paying taxes, goes directly back into this savings account. Any idle money that won't be needed in the foreseeable future should also be put into this savings account. At this stage in your life, this account should be a catch-all for money so you can start your savings and investment plan off with a bang.

This account should take the form of a basic savings account that earns interest. You want this money to be as liquid as possible so that when you do decide to invest it, it is readily available. Make sure to shop around for the highest interest rate you can find, while paying the lowest fees you can find.

The first $1000 of the savings account should be earmarked for the emergency fund we discussed earlier. Please remember that this is your emergency money and not your spending money. It is all too easy to dip into this money when you are short of funds, but if you hold off, you will be happier in the long run. After the first $1000 in this account, the rest is the money you will be investing.

The first stipulation about your savings account is that aside from the emergency fund money, no money should ever be taken out unless it is for the purpose of making an investment. Even if you're in a jam, don't give up your discipline and dip into it. If you do, it'll dramatically alter the overall plan we talked about in chapter thirteen, and you'll have to work much harder to get there.

The second stipulation refers back to the catch-all idea: that any and all after-tax income received from your investments should go directly back into the savings account to eventually be reinvested. This is the only way you will fully enjoy the magic of compounding, If you follow this second stipulation for at least ten straight years, you will become a very happy, disciplined, and responsible camper, and be well on your way to becoming a very wealthy camper too!

This savings account may start slowly at first because ten

percent of a young person's wage is not always a lot of money. Remember the catch-all idea, though, and do whatever you need to do (as long as it's legal!) to get started. Maybe you need to get a job doing something menial; maybe you are fortunate enough to be in a position to borrow your first $1000 from family. The point is to get started and stop making excuses!

I got started (and granted, I had some help) and in two years was able to produce an income for myself of over $10,000 a year from my investments prior to graduating from college! And mind you, that was investment income. It was income that was working *for* me, not money that I needed to go and physically work for to obtain. And it was income that I was able to earn over and above any income I received from the jobs I had along the way. This might seem a little complicated at first, but use your head and trust your gut. You've got this. Your results will be different from mine—every person's experience is, after all, unique—but you've got this!

A quick note: if you are able to take the borrowing route to start your savings account, it is important that you be responsible with that money and use it for investment purposes *only*, and pay it back *promptly*. If you do so successfully, not only will you be on the road to great financial health, but you will earn a positive reputation for yourself. If you don't, you put your financial future *and* your perceived reliability in jeopardy.

Anyway, that's the savings account. Now let's move on to the just-as-serious, but more recreational fun account.

FUN ACCOUNT (OTHERWISE KNOWN AS THE CHECKING ACCOUNT)

You MUST ALWAYS make sure that there is enough money left over to have plain-old fun. If you don't have fun with some of the money you make because you want to save it instead, you will quickly learn to hate saving money and may eventually give it up altogether. Using this leftover money to have fun is fabulous as long as you possess enough of the discipline we talked about earlier not to spend beyond your means. And remember once again, credit cards are *not* a substitute for the cash you don't have to go have fun with. This fun account—where the money you have earmarked for fun resides—is.

The fun account should take the form of a no-frills checking account. This is the account from which you will pay all your bills or debts, and whatever is left over is the money to go out and enjoy. I'm talking fun in the form of going out with friends, or buying yourself a new iPhone, or whatever other form of fun you want. I don't think I really need to tell you how to have fun. The older generation (of which I guess I'm part now) refers to leftover money as "discretionary income." I don't care what you choose to call it. Just be certain that you budget your bill-paying money so you will, in fact, have money left over to have fun with.

Simple enough, right? It really is. Most banking institutions have a low-to-no-cost checking account especially for students. Shop around and find one. This account usually doesn't earn interest (although some might), but there won't be a ton of money in this account, so that doesn't really matter. If you find that you do have extra cash in this account not earning interest, maybe you should put more money in your investment account.

I think I understand the concept of these two accounts, but it would be more understandable if you gave an example of exactly how these two accounts work.

Sure! Here we go…

A SCENARIO OF ACCOUNTS

If you decide to use the savings and fun account system, here is a scenario of what to do with your money when you get paid.

On payday, you get your paycheck of $300 direct deposited this way: at least $30 (10 percent of $300) into your savings account and the rest into your fun account. I say "at least" because you can always have more going into your savings account than the suggested 10 percent. Most employers and banks prefer direct deposit and will allow employees to designate how funds are deposited into multiple accounts. Setting it up ahead of time and automatically is the "set it and forget it" method I highly recommend.

You pay any monies you owe such as a credit card bill, a cell phone bill, etc., out of the fun account. The rest of the money in the fun account should hold you over until the next payday, when you get paid again. If you have extra money in your fun account, transfer some of it to your savings account.

When the savings account gets to about $1000, you should start looking for a sound investment for it. When the investment is made and you begin to receive some revenue from it, all—not some, but *all*—of that revenue needs to go right back into the savings account to be reinvested. After a while, the period between investments will shorten because you will be receiving revenue from past investments, plus the 10 percent of your pay, which you continue to deposit. The cool deal is part of the magic of compounding. If you keep up the good work, it only gets better and better over time.

Sounds great, Jason, but I don't get a $300 check every week. In fact, during the school year, I'm lucky if I make $50 a week from my part-time job at the pizza shop.

You've raised a valid point and it should be addressed as such. Although each person's scenario varies depending on their individual situation, this is about what should happen each week. I understand that all of you don't make $300 a week, especially if you're still in school. Just change the numbers to match your income. No amount is too small to save, and it's never too late or too early to start this routine.

Is it really that simple?

Yes, it is, because we are keeping things very fundamental. Remember K.I.S.S. (Keep It Simple, Stupid) from chapter six? The savings and fun account are the basics. They get you started into a savings and investment mode at a young age. Once you become comfortable with these accounts, you may find a need for others, such as a business account (if you have your own business) or an account specifically for school expenses, etc. You will know when you have these needs. Now the question is where to open these accounts.

WHERE TO LOOK

Let's examine the pros and cons of two different kinds of institutions: banks and credit unions. The four features we need to address while examining these institutions are convenience, price, service, and safety.

There are some questions you need to consider when you are shopping for places to open your accounts: Is the institution easily accessible to me and open when I need it? What rate does it offer and what fees does it charge? Does it take care of my needs and handle them in a pleasing manner? How safe will my money be?

BANKS

A VERY BROAD definition of a bank is an institution that has the ability and authority from the state or federal government to receive and pay interest on deposits and lend money on personal and/or real property.

Banks are very convenient, for the most part. They tend to have branches and/or ATMs around every block, and most banks have robust online capabilities.

Banks can be a bit pricier than credit unions. With that said, there are still many banks that offer very low-to-no-fee accounts. Outside of the student accounts offered by some banks (which can, but not always, include hidden charges), most of the fees for other accounts can be a heavy burden on your wallet. Many banks don't particularly like small accounts and will impose fees if your account drops below a certain amount, so be on the lookout for that language in their disclosures.

The key to getting good service at a bank is to find a small local one and go in to sit down with a manager to discuss your banking needs and goals with him/her. This is the real service test for banks, especially for young adults. If the manager is willing to sit down with a young adult to discuss and answer questions favorably, then chances are you will also be happy with the bank's ongoing services.

If you do decide to bank with them, every time you go in, make your presence known in a polite way and try to get on a first-name basis with the people who work there, especially the management and loan department. The relationships you are forming can help you when you need a car, house, or business loan.

My father built up just such a relationship with a local bank in our area. He was always on time with any payments he owed, and if any minor problems arose, he quickly took care of them. Over the years, he got to know the vice president of the bank well. So well, in fact, that whenever Dad needed a loan for investments or other purposes, he could just call the vice president and get it approved that day, instead of having to wait weeks like everyone else. The vice president kept blank approval forms with my father's name on them in his desk drawer. Now that's the relationship to have with a bank!

Banking and lending rules and laws have changed quite a bit over the years, so don't expect a bank to have blank approvals with your name on them floating around anywhere anymore. But creating relationships with banks still matters, even in today's fast-paced, virtual world.

The robust online services and convenience of some of the bigger banks might outweigh the small-town personal relationships that can be forged, as described above, with a smaller bank, so you'll need to identify which is more important to you as you shop around.

Each account at a bank is insured up to $250,000 by the Federal Deposit Insurance Corporation (FDIC), so your money is safe even if there is a challenge somewhere along the line.

Now on to credit unions and what they have to offer.

CREDIT UNIONS

Let me tell you up front, I love credit unions for certain products and situations and so should you! That's my opinion; now let me give you some facts about them.

Members of a credit union are supposed to have a common bond, such as working for the same employer, or living in the same neighborhood or community, or belonging to the same club. For this reason, some people believe that credit unions may not be as convenient as banks, but there are nearly 6,000 credit unions around the country. In other words, if you decide to belong to a credit union, you'll find one.

I have read that credit union service is not supposed to be as good as other institutions because of their small size, but I have experienced the exact opposite. The credit union I have belonged to since 1990, First Financial Federal Credit Union of Maryland, caters to my needs very well. They are as courteous as they can be with me. Whenever I have a question, I just call them or go online and am able to get an answer right away. They, like most other credit unions, offer just about as many services as banks do.

What about price?

Credit unions are nonprofit organizations, which means that, overall, their rates on interest-bearing accounts are usually higher, and their fees on accounts are usually lower, than banks. For example, my checking account with First Financial is a fun account as described above, so it is not interest-bearing. But in the past almost thirty years, I have been charged only seventy-five cents twice in fees to keep my account open. No monthly service charge, no fee per check, no minimum balance required, no fees at all! The only reason I was charged the seventy-five cents was because I used an ATM in another state (which they don't even care about anymore); otherwise there is no charge for using ATMs. Once you start shopping around, you'll find this is amazing pricing. The rates credit unions charge on automobile and home equity loans are also usually a little lower than that of other institutions. Overall, credit unions get an "A+" on their pricing when compared to other places you could put your money.

Credit union accounts are also insured up to $250,000 by the federally sponsored National Credit Union Administration, so the safety of your money is comparable to banks.

Here is what I have found after more than twenty-five years of personally using both banks and credit unions for certain accounts: they're both great!

When I was in college and for much of my young adult life, the credit union already mentioned served my needs very well for all the reasons mentioned above. It was perfect for my first savings and fun accounts and a few car and house loans over the years, and the service has always been top-notch. As I got older and my financial needs got more complicated, with multiple lending needs, business account requirements, etc., I needed to expand my horizons to a more full-service banking solution, which has also worked out very well. With any of the institutions at which I've banked over the years, the one thing that remained top priority for me was the relationship I had with the people working there. I've always found that when that relationship is tight, things tend to happen quicker and better.

So my personal conclusion is that both banks *and* credit unions are great, especially when you can establish a close relationship and use the institution for what it is best at providing.

Now you know what accounts you need, where to open those accounts, and what my personal experience has been over the years so…

START NOW!

What will YOU do as a result of reading this chapter?
YOUR Thoughts on Banking

CHAPTER FIFTEEN

CREDIT CARDS

Listed below are some important credit card terms that will be helpful to know while reading this chapter:

APR—Annual Percentage Rate, which is the relative cost of credit on a yearly basis. The Federal Truth-in-Lending Act requires all lenders to use APR when stating their interest rates so consumers can equally and fairly compare the different rates.

Balance—The amount you owe to the bank that issued the card. In other words, the sum of all the purchases with your credit card in a particular billing cycle, plus any unpaid balances from the previous billing cycles.

Billing Cycle—Usually, a 28-to-30-day period that marks the beginning and end of your billing period. The billing cycle does not necessarily coincide with the beginning or end of the month. At the end of each cycle, you receive a statement with your purchases listed on it.

Convenience Checks (or cash advance checks)—Checks that some banks issue you free of charge with your credit card. They can be used just like any other check. The amount of the check shows up with your statement at the end of the month, along with any purchases you have made with your card. Banks sometimes charge a higher interest rate on these checks than on regular charges on the card, along with cash advance fees, so be sure to read and understand the part of the credit card agreement that deals with this subject.

Credit Card Agreement—A document that explains the different policies that the bank follows with regard to its credit cards. Answers to many questions can be found here, although the language used in this document can be difficult to understand.

Credit Line or Limit—The most you can charge on your credit card at one time. Banks usually issue students a credit limit somewhere just under $1000. If you charge more than this amount, the bank will either charge you a penalty or the charge will be denied when you attempt to use the card.

Fixed Rate—Means the interest rate will stay the same. This is the opposite of a variable rate, which has the potential to change.

Interest (as applied to credit cards)—The amount, stated as the APR, you are charged if you don't pay off your balance by the payment due date on your statement. This can also be referred to as finance charges.

Statement—Bill you receive at the end of your billing cycle with the total of that billing cycle's purchases plus any unpaid balances, interest, and fees from the previous billing cycles.

OK, I got all the definitions. Now what?

Treat credit cards exactly as you would fire. They can be a great resource in times of need and if used with extreme caution, but one little slip-up and they are not forgiving. No joke here, people.

I can't state strongly enough how dangerous credit cards can be if not used properly. If you have even the slightest thought that you might get yourself into trouble with a credit card, please do not apply for one, at least not yet. But read this chapter to learn the reasons for concern.

"Like fire," "caution," "dangerous." Sounds like fun. Tell me more.

In this chapter I will outline the criteria you should watch for while looking for a credit card, along with suggestions on how to use it once you get approved for and obtain one. Then I will take you step by step through a credit card application so you will know exactly how to fill one out.

First, if you are not yet eighteen, you will have a difficult time being approved for a credit card (even a store card) unless one of your parents co-sign for you, which I do not recommend. The banks who issue these cards say they use a uniform code when selecting who gets a card and who doesn't. But through my research and personal experience, I have concluded that different banks have different criteria when choosing who gets approved for a credit card and who does not. Throughout my life I have been turned down flat for some credit cards and been given credit lines of up to $50,000 for others.

I first applied for and received a credit card when I was a freshman in college. My reasons for applying at that time were to use the card as an additional piece of identification and to have for use in emergency situations. I also wanted to establish my credit history.

It took a little time to convince my parents that these needs were valid because they were afraid I might abuse the privilege of possessing a credit card, charging things impulsively. I was so fearful that my parents might be correct that I hardly ever used my card for anything for the first couple of months.

After getting comfortable with the card, I began to use it on a regular basis, and before I knew it, I had proved my parents' concerns correct. I got a statement at the end of my freshman year in college that I was unable to pay from my spending account. I made a promise to myself right after opening that bill that never, *ever* would I make such a stupid mistake with a credit card again. Fortunately, a friend bailed me out of that horrible situation and helped me pay off the balance owed so I did not incur high finance charges, but I should never have gotten into that predicament in the first place.

And here is lesson #1 about credit cards that will be repeated throughout this chapter: Never, I mean *never, ever* charge something on a credit card that you do not have the cash for sitting in the bank in your spending account. Like *never*!

OK. I get it, credit cards are dangerous. What should I do not to make the same mistake you did?

I now look at a credit card as a convenient alternative to cash. As stated above, I have made a rule not to *ever* use one for spending purposes unless I am certain I have enough cash in the bank to cover whatever I am about to purchase. That way, when the statement comes at the end of the month, I know that I will have enough money to pay it in full. I would suggest that you also adopt this rule, and at this stage in your life, there should be no exceptions to it! Not even if you are going to get paid next week and won't receive the statement for a purchase you make today until a month from now. Why? Because although this thinking may work a few times, you will soon develop bad habits. Before you know it, you will receive a statement that you will not be able to pay. And that is exactly the point at which the bank that issued the credit card starts to take over some control of your finances—something that you do *not* want to have happen, especially so early in your life. Please learn from my mistake and don't make the same one yourself. That is what mistakes are for—to learn from. When you want to make a purchase with a card, first make sure that you have enough cash in your spending account to cover it and, secondly, earmark that money to pay your credit card bill so you won't use it for anything else.

Some people won't agree with this rule because they believe the whole purpose of a credit card is to make purchases when one needs something and then carry the balance until it is convenient to fully pay the bill. This would be a valid argument except for the outrageous interest rates they are being charged when they carry a balance from one month to the next. A quick Google search reveals many cards that charge interest rates as high as 25 percent! I thought only loan sharks and skilled businesspeople could charge and/or receive that kind of rate. It would be almost impossible to get ahead financially once you were forced to pay such high interest rates. I hope none of you are ever in a position where you need money so badly you are willing to pay 25 percent for it. For example, I'll bet you that your parents or Aunt Lucy (and doesn't everyone have an Aunt Lucy?) will loan you money at less than 25 percent a year.

I use the term "loan" because that is exactly what the banks who issue these cards do. They loan you money every time you make a purchase with your card. You are not required to pay that loan back to the bank until you receive the statement in the mail with that particular purchase on it. Even then, the due date for payment of the bill is sometimes three or three and a half weeks away. So, you usually have at least thirty days from when you make a purchase using a credit card to when you actually have to pay for it. For most regular purchases, interest does not start accruing until after that due date. If you pay the bill by the due date, you are receiving a thirty-day, interest-free loan. It's like free money, and if you think about it, that's a great deal!

You can even extend this loan to almost two months if you make your purchase right after your statement date. You won't receive your next statement for about a month, and then you'll have another three to three and a half weeks until it's due. Not too many other people or businesses will offer that kind of deal. Try going to a hot dog stand and after ordering your dog, telling the vendor that you will gladly pay for it in thirty days. You can be certain that the vendor will snatch your hot dog away from you just as fast as he gave it to you.

As long as you stick to paying your bill in full each month, you will always have free use of the bank's money for about a month. Therefore, while you shop around for cards (and you *should* shop around and compare, which can be done easily online), don't worry about what the interest rate is, because if you follow our rule, you are never going to have to pay it anyway.

Instead, look for a card that has little or no annual fee. If you find one with no annual fee and you pay your bill on time every month, not only will you enjoy the convenience and benefits of an interest-free loan, you will also start to build a nice credit history for yourself that will be super helpful when you go to purchase your first car or house.

WARNING!

To ENJOY THE great benefits mentioned above, you must possess an enormous amount of self-discipline. Loading up purchases on credit cards and not paying for them at the end of the month is something too many people do, and it is an easy trap to fall into. In fact, a recent study showed that credit card holders ages twenty-three and under carry month-to-month balances of over $2,000! And according to a 2017 Federal Reserve report, 55 percent of Americans carry a credit card balance from month to month (https://www.creditdonkey.com/average-credit-card-debt.html). Wow!

I would hate for you to obtain a high-interest card just because it has a low or no annual fee, and then get stuck paying that high interest because you lacked the self-discipline to make sure you had sufficient funds to pay your bill. Do *not* become part of the 55 percent! Remember, the only reason for you not to worry about the interest rate on a credit card is if you plan to follow our rule of paying your bill in full, each and every month. End of warning.

CREDIT HISTORY

I CAN'T EMPHASIZE how important it is for you to view credit card use as a privilege. If you look at your credit use this way and treat the privilege with respect—namely, by paying your bill on time each month and not using your card to make purchases you don't already have the cash for—your future will benefit greatly. Your credit use over time makes for a clean credit history, which is essential to have a successful financial future—it's like that, and that's the way it is.

After spending twenty-one years as a mortgage banker, I can tell you story after story of people who otherwise seemed credit-worthy due to their savings and income data, but were turned down for housing loans because they were not able to pay their bills on time. Your first credit card represents what is likely to be the beginning of your life's credit history, and if you heed my advice about paying your credit card bill (and all your bills) on time, every time, your credit history will reflect only good things about your personal credit-worthiness. This will continue to create financial options for you in the journey of life.

I don't know about you, but I certainly don't want the purchase of my dream house held up because I still owe $65 on some bill I didn't pay enough attention to. Get my drift? You may feel that I am overdoing this issue a bit, but I have seen too many people get into serious trouble with credit cards over the years. And this type of trouble has such major implications to a person's financial future. You've probably got it by this point, though.

BACK TO BASICS

Make sure that from the time you fill out an application for a credit card to when you receive your statement at the end of the month, you read all documents carefully. This prevents you from running into unexpected costs or surprises of any kind. You should make a habit of this precautionary measure with *all* your documents, especially the ones you have to sign.

Another idea is to call or chat online with the bank's customer service as soon as you have a question of any kind about your card. Some service centers are pleasant to deal with and others not so much, but don't let them put you off. If, when you get off the phone or end the chat, you are still confused about something, call/chat with them again. When you do speak with someone at the service center, always get the name of the person you are speaking with and write that name down, along with the date you spoke to them. That way you'll have a reference, or paper trail, if you ever need to call back or refer to your conversation. Each bank sets its own policies about how they handle problems and price discrepancies with their credit cards, and all of this will be provided to you, both on their website and snail mailed to you. Make sure to actually read what is sent to you.

REWARDS

Great places for you to start looking for and comparing cards to find the best credit card for you are:

www.comparecards.com
www.wallethub.com
www.thepointsguy.com

Researching and finding the right card for you and your needs are important. One thing you may be interested in is that many cards come with rewards that can include points towards purchases, cash back, or miles/points/dollars toward air travel. In fact, one of our young adult editors, who is a pro at researching and using cards with rewards, was able to travel to Europe twice and the Caribbean once, and he "flew all over the US essentially for free using credit card points" during his first three years out of college. That may be the kind of thing you want to check out yourself.

My own experience with a cash-back credit card has been very positive. It enabled me to directly pay down one of our mortgages to the tune of over $15,000 over the years. I mean, some of these rewards cards are crazy good.

With that being said, many cards that offer rewards have annual fees, and that may or may not be something you want to get into. It really depends on your needs, but I did want to include the information on rewards to make you aware of them.

THE APPLICATION

Now that you know most of the dos and don'ts of possessing a credit card, along with the benefits of having one, let's learn how to fill out an application to receive one in the first place. On most college campuses, credit cards are advertised in every nook and cranny the banks can think of, and of course you can always find one online.

As you'll see, everything is fairly straightforward. I don't think any of the questions on the application will trip you up, but let me explain why some of them are asked.

First, banks want your social security number because they use it to obtain your credit report from a credit bureau. (*Please be extremely cautious about entering your social security number anywhere online!* Make sure you are working on an application from a reputable company, using a secure website with an SSL Certificate.) Your social security number is your identification number when it comes to credit. Most of you won't have much, if any, credit history for them to check simply because you've never had credit before, unless you have a student loan. And in this case, that's going to be OK.

Banks want to know what school you attend and what year you are in. The higher your class level, the more favorable it is for you. Banks figure the higher your level, the more responsible you are, though there are many, including myself, who would beg to differ on this point.

Your employer's name and your annual income help the bank decide whether or not they think you can afford the card. Some banks will accept income from allowances or from scholarships in place of employment income.

The banking references section on the application gives the bank some indication of your financial responsibility. By signing the bottom of the application you are not only giving the bank authority to obtain a credit report on you, but also to check your banking references to verify and check balances in your accounts.

Again, most of the questions on the application are straightforward, but if you have any questions while you are filling one out, don't hesitate to call or chat with the bank's customer service reps.

DISCLOSURES

Most application brochures contain a disclosures section, and there are a number of things I want you to be on the lookout for there.

Most disclosures tend to appear in exceptionally fine print. Just a word of caution: Whenever you see fine print during your life, read it carefully, because it usually says something very important and can sometimes contain information that people are trying to slip by you.

The first thing to look for is the APR, or annual percentage rate. Let's say your disclosure form states that this particular card has an annual percentage rate on purchases of 19.8 percent. Wow! I told you that some banks charge extremely high rates. I certainly would rather go without a certain purchase than pay that high an interest rate. Next, you'll see that you won't be charged this high interest rate if you pay your bill on time each month. But note that you are charged interest from the *time of purchase* if you haven't paid the balance in full the month before. So it really does make a difference if you pay your balance in full each month (which we've already agreed that you will be doing *every single month*, right?).

The bank in our example computes interest by taking the average balance you've carried from day to day during your billing cycle and then charges you the 19.8 percent APR on that balance. Each bank uses a different system for computing the interest they charge, so make sure you understand that section on the disclosure form.

Then maybe you'll find that the annual fee for the use of this card is $18. And, finally, you'll learn about all the transaction fees this bank charges, such as foreign currency exchange fees and, of course, late fees. Make sure you understand these fees as well, because if you don't, they will sneak up on you and appear on your bill one month and cost you. These fees account for millions of dollars in revenues each year for the banks that issue credit cards, so you can bet that if you don't watch out, you will end up paying a couple of them yourself.

GO AHEAD—GIVE IT A TRY

If, after wading through this chapter, you feel you can responsibly handle the privilege of possessing a credit card, go out and find one that suits your particular needs. Don't fill out an application immediately. I would rather you shop around for one using the websites I've referenced above. If you search hard enough, you'll be able to find one with no annual fee, lots of rewards, and great customer service. Once you receive your card, please, please, *please* don't abuse it. If you treat the card with respect, like anything else, it will serve you well in the long run.

START NOW!

What will YOU do as a result of reading this chapter?
YOUR Thoughts on Credit Cards

SECTION FOUR:

FINAL THOUGHTS

CHAPTER SIXTEEN

LAST FEW SECRETS

WE'RE ALMOST AT the end, but there are just a few more secrets I would like to share with you before calling it quits. Some of them are financial secrets and some of them are more general secrets to help you out during the course of your life—you know, "well-being" secrets. I call them secrets because many of them I would not know myself if it weren't for either messing something up a whole lot or having someone pull me aside to tell them to me personally.

FINANCIAL SECRETS:

1. **Ensure all savings are on autopilot.** Remember the K.I.S.S. Method from chapter six? Most employers and banks/credit unions will give you the ability to have deposits made automatically straight into a savings or investing account. Start this auto savings now and never turn it off—you'll be surprised how quickly this adds up, between you contributing a little bit (say 10 percent of your income) and the magic of compounding we spoke about in chapter thirteen.

2. **Spend less than you make.** We've touched on this in a few different places, but I cannot state this point strongly enough. Debt will stifle and stress you to the max. Avoid it and live free.

3. **Make sure you are the only one who has control of your money!** You are the one who knows best what you want to do with your money, so don't let anybody have control of it except you. This includes family members and close friends.

4. **Keep your eyes and ears open at all times.** You never know what you are going to come across during the course of a day, especially when it touches on investment and business opportunities, so be certain to always be aware of what is happening around you.

5. **Keep good records.** I know I've already told you this once, but it is so important that I thought I would mention it again.

6. **Don't accumulate idle cash.** Having $2000 in your mattress does you no good. If this money is in a bank account, at least it is earning some interest. Don't delay in depositing checks or cash. Money just lying around is dangerous for two reasons: It can be lost, stolen, or forgotten about, and it serves as an unneeded temptation to spend.

7. **Don't prepay your bills.** You are penalized only if you don't pay your bills on time and you are usually not rewarded for paying them early. Paying early only decreases the time your money can earn interest. And as long as you pay your bills on time, your credit rating will be A-OK.

8. **Knowledge is key.** You'll never know all there is to know about money, so realize it and become a lifelong student on the subject. It's been said that if you think education is too expensive, try ignorance instead.

9. **As far as student loans go, I'd prefer that you stay as far away from them as you possibly can.** *The Wall Street Journal* reports that the average student loan debt per borrower is over $35,000, and when I was in the mortgage industry, I regularly saw people who were strapped with over $100,000 in student loans. This kind of debt burden is avoidable with creativity and work which, while it can be hard, is certainly not as hard as the emotional and financial toll debt like this can take on you.

   Some of the creative ways to avoid student loan debt are scholarships, community colleges, and part time jobs or side hustles to help pay for school. I understand that student loans are not one hundred percent avoidable in all circumstances and that each person's situation is unique. But I wanted you to know that there are much better alternatives. One of the best resources I've come across on this topic is Anthony O'Neal's work called *Debt Free Degree.* On his website, www.anthonyoneal.com, you will find all kinds of resources to help you earn a degree without having to finance it through loans.

   If you're reading this secret and you already have student loan debt, I want to tell you that you're going to be OK. You'll need to *start now* with a plan for that debt, but I'm here to encourage you that you have what it takes to manage it. A great place to start is right here: https://www.daveramsey.com/blog/how-to-pay-off-student-loans-quickly.

WELL-BEING SECRETS:

1. **Be you and no one else.** There is literally only one of you in this world forever, and all of history. You are wonderfully

and uniquely made; you are more than enough just the way you are, and only you can provide your amazingness to the world. You only need to aspire to be your best self and you will crush.

2. **Only take what you need in life.** There is no need for excess. Excess is for hogs, and who wants to be a hog? When you do take, make sure to leave something on the table so when the next person comes along, there is something left for them. The English philosopher John Locke said it best when he wrote, "He that leaves as much as another can make use of, does as good as take nothing at all."

3. **Pack lightly.** Similar to #2, but slightly different. You do not need as much as you think you might, and you certainly don't need as much as the people you see on social media.

4. **Social media is real life.** By now you've heard all the "once you post it, it's there forever" type of warnings, but as someone who has hired and fired people over the years, I can personally verify that employers will indeed check out your social media accounts prior to making hiring decisions. We are close to the day when our entire lives will be recorded, but for now, we have the choice about what we post and what we don't—please choose wisely.

5. **Pay more attention to your friends than your things.** Things collect dust and will disappoint you over time, every time. Your friends are amazing, don't collect dust, and get even better with age when you give them your attention.

6. **Look people in the eye when you talk to them.** This is such a lost but worthy skill. It shows honesty and integrity when you look someone in the eye while speaking with them. Please practice this skill. It is invaluable.

7. **Learn and remember peoples' names.** Dale Carnegie has said that the sweetest sound to someone's ear is to hear his or her own name. Think about how much you like it when someone you haven't seen for a long time remembers your name. If you have trouble remembering names, think of tricks to help you, such as writing them down or associating the names with something easily remembered. There are many recall techniques (Google "how to best remember names"); find the one that works best for you.

8. **Attack decisions and get them over with.** And once you've made a decision, don't look back and be wishy-washy about it. Stick with it.

9. **Never rule out daydreaming.** Daydreaming facilitates creativity. Losing creativity means losing some of our identity. So put the phone down and daydream away.

10. **Put yourself in their shoes.** Anytime you have a conflict with someone or don't understand why they are acting or thinking a certain way, mentally put yourself in their position. If humbly done, with intention, you will usually find that your mind is a lot more open to the situation, allowing you to better understand what is going on.

11. **Do what you fear.** This one may sound weird or difficult, and it is, but think about it. If you do, or even attempt to do, what scares you, over time, not much will.

12. **Work your ass off.** Whatever it is you want to do or achieve—know it's going to take a lot of work and it's going to be hard at times. That's OK. In fact, it's even to be expected. Right where it gets really hard, like not just reading-about-it kind of hard, but the kind of hard that brings you to tears and self-doubt and that feeling that it's not worth it—where you ultimately want to go is right around the corner from that place, so keep on going and work harder at it.

13. **Go to the right place for advice.** If you want advice on how to become a police officer, ask a police officer. If you need advice on money or investing, go to someone who is has vast experience in successfully handling their personal finances. In other words, go to the right source for advice, and don't mess around with someone who isn't really knowledgeable about, or who lacks experience in, the subject for which you are seeking advice.

14. **Say "thank you."** This is so easy to do, yet many people go entire days without saying those sweet words. People love to be appreciated. Every single day of your life you have something to be thankful for, so thank somebody for it. If you can't think of anything for which you are thankful on a particular day, call your parents or God and thank them for your existence!

15. **Consider what is the highest and best use of your time in each moment.** There will always be more to be done than you are able to do, more requests than you can fulfill. Make the decision right here and now to let go of all that noise. This precious life of yours is only happening once—there is no do-over—and once today is gone, it's gone forever.

Make the most of today, and stop rethinking yesterday and worrying about tomorrow. *Today* is the only day that matters today.

16. **Put the phone down.** This relates to the secret above, and I'm sure you've heard enough on this topic from your parents and your teachers to make your ears bleed, but here's my version: Put the phone down, look into people's eyes while you're face to face in real time, and have a conversation. You'll both be better for the experience.

17. **Make others feel good.** People might not remember what you say, but they will remember how you make them feel. So make 'em feel good.

18. **Use YouTube, podcasts, Audible, etc., as your personal library.** Some may charge but you can learn almost anything you want to learn about in the world for free on many of these platforms.

19. **Show up.** Eighty percent of life is simply showing up, so be there—even when you don't feel like it.

20. **The higher your emotional intelligence, the more success you'll have.** My observations over the years have made it abundantly clear to me that emotional stability and emotional intelligence is something that can and should be learned, honed, and then learned some more to obtain any modicum of success, however you define it.

21. **Pay attention to your physical and mental health now...**
    ...or you will later. I 1000 percent assure you that sometime in your life, you will pay a whole lot of attention

to your health. For most of us, it's a choice we can make. We either proactively pay attention to it by doing things daily like eating clean, moving our bodies, sleeping well, meditating, and laughing with others. Or we'll make the choice to *reactively* pay attention to our health by visiting a lot of doctors, inconveniencing our loved ones and spending a lot of money attempting to fix an unhealthy lifestyle.

22. **Start small, but start now!**

23. **Lastly—As I've said before, if you help enough people get what they want in life, you most assuredly will get what you want.** I first learned this secret from the late, great grandfather of everything motivational, Zig Ziglar. Thank you, Zig! If you only take away one idea from this book, let it be this last one. It will help you become a fulfilled person in this large world of ours.

START NOW!

What will YOU do as a result of reading this chapter?
YOUR Thoughts on Last Thoughts

CHAPTER SEVENTEEN

STANDING ON THE SHOULDERS OF GIANTS

"If I have seen further than others, it is by standing on the shoulders of giants."

—ISAAC NEWTON

THE BEST SAYINGS encapsulate big ideas in just a few words. They inspire, motivate, and encourage in a way that's hard to forget. Here are some sayings I have found helpful to me along the road of life. If nothing else, they should give you something to think about. I don't know the origins of some of them, but what's important is that you also have the opportunity to see further than others.

The secret to getting ahead is getting started.—Mark Twain

The difficult we do immediately. The impossible takes a little longer.—Dr. James E. Abell (yes, this is my dad)

All of us, at certain times in our lives, need to take advice and receive help from other people.—Alexis Carrel

Life is 10% what happens to us and 90% how we react to it.—Dennis P. Kimbro

Life is really simple, but we insist on making it complicated. —Confucius

You change your life by changing your heart.—Max Lucado

If your life goes along too easily, you become soft.—Dalai Lama

The only real failure in life is the failure to try.—George Bernard Shaw

The more you praise and celebrate your life, the more there is in life to celebrate.—Oprah Winfrey

Life is not a matter of milestones, but of moments.—Rose Kennedy

The most important conversations we have every day are with ourselves.

Education is the one thing that no one can take from you.—B.B. King

Acquire the best you can find, and take care of it so it lasts forever.

One who fears failure limits his activities. Failure is only the opportunity to more intelligently begin again.—Henry Ford

Any fool can work for a living. Invest your money.

Love people, use things.

You can't wait around for the breaks in your life, you have to go out and make them happen.

Twenty years from now you will be more disappointed by the things that you didn't do than by the ones you did do.—Mark Twain

Don't dwell on short-term failures. Ponder instead your long-term goals. Success is getting what you want; Happiness is wanting what you get.—Dale Carnegie

On time is late for leaders.—paraphrase of Eric Jerome Dickey

I don't care if you sell apples on the street corner, but make sure you sell the best damn apples there are.

Take time for friendship; it is the source of happiness.

To grow a beautiful rose you have to get your hands in a little manure.

It's only work if you would rather be doing something else.—Pauline Phillips (aka Abigail Van Buren, or "Dear Abby")

Do not, for any reason, simply do not be ashamed to say, "I do not understand."

People don't care how much you know—until they know how much you care.—Theodore Roosevelt

Everyone in life has a purpose, even if it's to serve as a bad example.—Carroll Bryant

We're not primarily put upon this earth to see through one another, but to see one another through. —Peter DeVries

You can't catch any fish if you don't put your bait in the water.

Never do anything halfway.

Make sure that every morning when you get up, you can stand to look at yourself in the mirror.

Now is the time of your life. Enjoy it to the fullest.

To change is difficult; not to change is fatal. —William Pollard

Education is cheap compared to ignorance.

Always do right. That will gratify some of the people, and astonish the rest. —Mark Twain

What I do today is important because I am exchanging a day of my life for it. —Heartsill Wilson

If you find a path with no obstacles, it probably doesn't lead anywhere. —Frank A. Clark

People who ask, get what they want.

Be an individualist. He who follows another is always behind.

Someday is not a day of the week.

It is not what we take up but what we give up that makes us rich. —Henry Ward Beecher

Money is a terrible master but an excellent servant.—P. T. Barnum

Every expert started out the same way—by learning the basics.

It takes both rain and sunshine to make a rainbow.

Losers let it happen; winners make it happen.—Denis Waitley

No journey is too long if you find what you're looking for.

We are advertised by our loving friends.—Shakespeare

Do what you fear. Do what scares you—then nothing will.—Roger Dawson

Regarding your long-term goals—don't just cross those bridges when you come to them or burn them after you traverse them. Instead, devise a plan of action to successfully reach and enjoy crossing those bridges and lay out a red carpet for those who may need to take the same bridge.

Your only limitations should be your dreams.

Anyone who says they never had a chance never took a chance.

You don't treat people like people to make a sale, you treat people like people 'cause it's the right thing to do.

Success and happiness, like most things, are relative.

Never, ever be ashamed of where you come from or what you do or don't have.

It's not how much money you make, but how much money you keep, how hard it works for you, and how many generations you keep it for.—Robert Kiyosaki

The grass is not always greener on the other side.

Sometimes you just need to put your yes on the table.—Mitchel Lee

If an idea has a WOW in it, it will happen—unless you abandon it.—Robert Schuller

Too many people spend money they earned... to buy things they don't want... to impress people that they don't like.—Will Rogers

A wise person should have money in their head, but not in their heart.—Jonathan Swift

Wealth consists not in having great possessions, but in having few wants.—Epictetus

Every day is a bank account, and time is our currency. No one is rich, no one is poor, we've got 24 hours each.—Christopher Rice

Annual income twenty pounds, annual expenditure nineteen six, result happiness. Annual income twenty pounds, annual expenditure twenty pound ought and six, result misery.—Charles Dickens

Opportunity is missed by most people because it is dressed in overalls and looks like work.—Thomas Edison

Formal education will make you a living; self-education will make you a fortune.—Jim Rohn

Financial peace isn't the acquisition of stuff. It's learning to live on less than you make, so you can give money back and have money to invest. You can't win until you do this.—Dave Ramsey

He who loses a friend, loses much more; he who loses faith, loses all.—Eleanor Roosevelt

Try to save something while your salary is small; it's impossible to save after you begin to earn more.—Jack Benny

Every time you borrow money, you're robbing your future self.—Nathan W. Morris

Rich people have small TVs and big libraries, and poor people have small libraries and big TVs.—Zig Ziglar

Wealth is not his that has it, but his that enjoys it.—Benjamin Franklin

If you tell the truth, you don't have to remember what you said.—Mark Twain

The habit of saving is itself an education; it fosters every virtue, teaches self-denial, cultivates the sense of order, trains to forethought, and so broadens the mind.—T. T. Munger

We make a living by what we get, but we make a life by what we give.—Winston Churchill

It's not the situation, but how we react or respond to the situation that's important.—Zig Ziglar

Courage is being scared to death, but saddling up anyway.—John Wayne

Let no feeling of discouragement prey upon you, and in the end you are sure to succeed.—Abraham Lincoln

If your ship doesn't come in, swim out to meet it!—Jonathan Winters

You got to be lean to go into the jungle.—Judy Miles

When you're ahead don't complain and when you're behind negotiate.—Dr. James E. Abell

Screw it, Let's do it!—Richard Branson

START NOW!

AFTERWORD

You have reached the end of this book. Congratulations! I hope your adventure through it has been both enjoyable and productive. As I said in the introduction, if you are able to take even one concept from it and apply it to your life or allow it to spark your own concepts or ideas, this book has served the purpose for which it was written.

I tried to write this book in the same manner as I would casually speak with a friend. I wanted the concepts to come to you as easily and clearly as possible. If there is even one sentence in it that you do not fully understand, hit me up on Twitter @rewirejason or on LinkedIn at https://www.linkedin.com/in/rewirejason/.

It has been proved that one of the best ways to teach others is through example. Throughout this book, I have supplied anecdotes from my own life, some successful and some otherwise, to serve as examples for you. It is my hope that from my stories you have been able to learn what works while avoiding a pothole or two on your own journey. Now I call on you to do the same.

As a young adult, you must realize that you are not only the leaders of tomorrow, but the leaders of today—*if* you choose to be. At the very least, you are the leaders of your own lives, which is really quite powerful. Remember that no matter what you do during your lifetime, you should be happy with yourself in doing it. Not happy in terms of my standards or your parents' or your friends' or society's, but happy by your own standards. My best wishes are with you always and good luck with everything you do!

ACKNOWLEDGMENTS

Just like the first go around with this book I've gotta give it up to my parents, Esten and Sis Abell, who as part of America's Greatest Generation successfully combined two families in Brady Bunch fashion with unparalleled craziness and excellence. And then they had me—and I had this book!

My wife is a complete piece of work which is exactly what I need to complete projects like *Start Now*. Amy, without you in my life encouraging me, making me laugh daily, and loving me the way you, do this book just doesn't happen.

Julia and JJ, our children, not only helped in editing the book you hold in your hands, but also provided a private lens for me to see what it's really like to be a young adult today. It ain't easy and both of you are navigating life with an individualism and greatness that I marvel at daily.

Without the inspiration of Jim Napier on an impressionable 19-year-old boy in the summer of '90, the original version of this book would never have happened—and subsequently neither would this version.

My Chief Editor—the unflinching wordsmith calm to my crazy "let's write that book again" storm. Thank you, Steph, for your organized patience and mad publishing skills.

My peers at Rewire who appropriately pointed out the irony of my two-year procrastination in authoring a book titled *Start Now*, while at the same time gently encouraging the project. This book has been enhanced by each of you. Thank you to Steve, Paolo, Longan, and Raffa.

The other six young adult editors who were delicately rough on me with their "we really don't think your examples about pagers and floppy disks are that up to date" while also being instrumental in ensuring the book is relevant and valuable to you: Charlie Miller, Chris Campbell, Rees Draminski,

Hannah Ruby, Payton Lookenbill, and Ashley Rhoten.

My "Iron Sharpens Iron" boys who straighten me out when I drift and hold me accountable to book projects and stuff: Wolfy, Footy, Heej, Kling, Doctor, Double R, and Vin.

Without enthusiastic crazies letting the world know about a book like this, no one ends up reading it. Thanks to the best launch team in the world: Neddy Abell, Tim Abell, Michael Addison, Glenn Astolfi, Matt Auman, Jennifer Balzano, Pam Bateman, Debbie Benkert, Michael Bergin, Vikas Bhatia, Raquel Borras, Pat Bowman, Timothy Brown, Laura Calandrella, Walter Cawley, Maria Ciarrocchi, Zachary Cochran, Cassandra Compton, Terri Donaldson, Jen Doyle, Mike Doyle, Jenn Farrer, Stephen Feron, Tracie Feron, Douglas Fields, Jessica Fields, Scott Fields, Adam Foote, Haley Garcia, Chad Gerlt, Erin Gerlt, Trent Gladstone, Michael Gleeson, Raj Goyal, Joel Graybeal, Kathleen Grieve, Rob Harvey, Stacia Hejeebu, Bruce Hohensee, Jim Hunter, Robert Jandrasits, Tina Jarvis, Bob Kaestner, Rick Kellow, Brendan Kelly, Brian Kelly, Kim Kettering, Mander Kiang, Dave Krueger, Mitchel Lee, Sophia Malpocker, Mike Mcbride, Ryan Miller, Miguel Miranda, Jay Morton, Greg Murach, Tommy Myers, Ryan Niles, Jenny Penley, Leo Pepper, Kathy Petersen, Jerry Rader, Edie Raphael, Devin Reinhold, Daniel Reyes, John Reyes, Renee Reyes, Aaryn Richardson, Ryan Richardson, John Rogers, Tony Sheng, Daniel Shin, Kenneth Slezak, Shaun Smithson, Andrea Solan, Kirk Stensrud, Rick Trott, Dominic Turano, Stuart Tyrie, Sheila Vaughan, Mike Walton, Pam Warburton, Peggy Wolf, Jimmy Woo, Rich Yauger, Elizabeth Yost, Dustin Youngstrom, and Kevin Youngstrom.

ABOUT THE AUTHOR

Jason Abell is a speaker, author and business coach at Rewire, a coaching company he helped start in 2014. Rewire's clients include cool companies like Under Armour, Nike, Chick-fil-A, and Wells Fargo.

Jason wrote the first edition of *Start Now* while still in college, and currently, he is a regular podcast guest, still writes a bunch, and eats more salads than he used to.

He is passionate about helping others which led him and his wife Amy to found Sadie's Gift, a non-profit that has raised almost a million bucks for the Johns Hopkins Children's Center. And this passion is behind The Buck-A-Book Movement, which will donate $1 for every copy of *Start Now* purchased to the National Alliance on Mental Illness.

Jason lives in Baltimore with his wife and two kids, thinks people are cool, laughs at himself a lot, and loves family and the outdoors.

rewireinc.com/startnow
linkedin.com/in/rewirejason
twitter: @rewirejason
facebook.com/rewirejason

WHAT DID YOU THINK OF START NOW?

First of all, thank you for purchasing and reading this book. I know you could have picked any number of books to read, but you picked this one and for that I am extremely grateful.

I hope that it added value and quality to your life. If so, it would be great if you could share this book with your friends and family by posting about it on your socials.

You would be doing me a huge solid if you took some time to post a review on Amazon. Your feedback and support will help me greatly improve my writing for future projects and make this book even better. A typical Amazon review takes about five minutes to submit and it helps future readers forever. **Not a bad trade!**

BUCK A BOOK MOVEMENT

Too many young adults suffer from mental illness. The topic needs to be brought out of the dark and addressed with science and love.

There are a lot of really smart people working on this and you just become one of them!

With every copy of Start Now purchased, **$1 will be donated to the National Alliance on Mental Illness.**

THANK YOU!